MAXIMISING YC

SELF-DEVELOPMENT

MAXIMISING YOUR MEMORY

How to train yourself to remember more

Peter Marshall

How To Books

Cartoons by Mike Flanagan

British Library Cataloguing in Publication Data
A catalogue record for this book is available from the British Library.

© Copyright 1998 by Peter Marshall.

First published by How To Books Ltd, 3 Newtec Place,
Magdalen Road, Oxford OX4 1RE, United Kingdom.
Tel: (01865) 793806. Fax: (01865) 248780.

Note: The material contained in this book is set out in good faith for
general guidance and no liability can be accepted for loss or expense
incurred as a result of relying in particular circumstances on statements
made in the book. The laws and regulations are complex and liable to
change, and readers should check the current position with the relevant
authorities before making personal arrangements.

Produced for How To Books by Deer Park Productions.
Typeset by PDQ Typesetting, Stoke-on-Trent, Staffs.
Printed and bound by Cromwell Press, Trowbridge, Wiltshire.

Contents

Preface   9

Foreword   11

1 Why enhance your memory?   13

Benefiting professionally   13
Excelling educationally   14
Being accepted socially   15
Developing personally   17
Summary   18
Discussion points   19

2 What do we know about memory?   20

How much can it hold?   20
What aspects of memory are there?   20
How does memory work?   21
The ways memory can fail   24
Testing memory   26
What is good for memory?   27
The serial reproduction effect   28
Natural rhythm   28
Choosing the right technique   30
Summary   31
Discussion points   32

3 Putting the material in   33

Being selective and orderly   33
Organising the environment for studying   38
Interacting with existing knowledge   40
Using mnemonics   43
Summary   46
Discussion points   46

4 Keeping it there 47

Testing regularly 47
Reprocessing frequently 48
Talking about it 51
Thinking about it periodically 52
Using physical memory aids 53
Summary 56
Discussion points 56

5 Getting it out 57

Remembering the structure 57
Going through the alphabet 59
Recalling shapes 59
Looking for cues 61
Thinking around 62
Relaxing 64
Leaving it to the unconscious 65
Computing 66
Reconstructing 67
Summary 68

6 Chunking 70

What is chunking? 70
Using acronyms 71
Using catchphrases 72
Using shapes 73
Summary 76

7 Associating 77

What is association? 77
Pegging to images 79
Using method of loci 99
The number shape system 100
The number rhyme system 101
The alphabet system 102
Building images into pictures 103
Remembering telephone numbers 105
Remembering historical dates 106
Learning languages 107
Memorising long numbers 107
Card memory 109
Spelling 110
Summary 112
Discussion points 112

8   Using memory techniques sensibly   113

Learning effectively   113
What memory techniques can't do   115
What memory techniques can do   116
Summary   117
Discussion points   118

Further reading   119

Index   121

LIST OF ILLUSTRATIONS

1.   Studygram for remembering aspects of production   34
2.   Shapes useful for chunking in a studygram   45

Preface

We agonised over the title of this book – publisher, copy editor and I. We considered the titles *Developing Your Memory, Improving Your Memory* and *Boosting Your Memory.*

The trouble with each of these was they seemed to imply that a person's basic memory ability can be changed. At the biological level this is not so. However, as I pointed out in my last book on mind development, *How to Study and Learn,* you may not be able to alter the hardware you have, but you can do a lot with the software. Our brains are our hardware, and the routines we learn are our software.

There are other memory books on the market: what is unique about this one is that it makes no wild claims that a person's fundamental memory ability can be altered – it cannot. What it does claim, however, is that you can greatly increase your ability to store, retain and recall things by learning to support your memory with other trained cognitive abilities. Thus *Maximising* was the word we chose to use in the title.

Boosting was particularly inappropriate, since it suggested only a marginal increase – 'a few percent', perhaps. But this book will teach you how to increase your ability to remember things not just by a margin, but many-fold.

A powerful ability to store, retain and recall relevant information brings obvious advantages in career, educational, social and personal terms.

At school and college those certificates which provide a passport to a career depend heavily on what you can remember in the exam room. Once in the world of work, being able to recall details which slip the minds of your colleagues will give you a competitive edge. In addition, one of the secrets of being popular with customers and friends is to remember their names and the little things which make them feel they matter to you. This book shows you how you can achieve it.

Peter Marshall

Foreword

When I was introduced to Peter Marshall I was a raw young man with a talent for remembering things so great it perplexed me. I was, at the time, using it to make a living doing shows at Blackpool, demonstrating my memory for remembering telephone numbers. Peter took an immediate interest in my ability and before I knew it he was delving into not only my techniques, but my childhood conditions, to discover what led me to develop in such a way. His keen investigative nature leaves no stone unturned.

In addition to his research interests, he was also interested in my own development. It was he who persuaded me to educate myself in the subject, so that I could understand my memory talents. It was he who persuaded me to change from working with telephone numbers to memorising the *Pi* constant. It was he who served as chief invigilator in my two televised attempts to get into the *Guinness Book of Records* for this.

Peter is one of the most knowledgeable and inspiring authorities of the present time on the subject of mind development. Much of his life has been selflessly devoted to helping other people to improve themselves. There are many I know personally, and many more I do not, who owe a debt of gratitude to him for changing their lives forever. He made them see they can expect better things in life. He made them see they were capable of great things. To these people, Peter Marshall is a dream-maker – one who not only builds people's dreams, but also shows them how to make them come true.

He has a talent for making the difficult easy, for simplifying things. This book is no exception. Indeed, it is all I expected it to be: clear, comprehensive and inspiring. I thoroughly recommend it.

Tom Morton
Popular TV mnemomist

1
Why Enhance Your Memory?

Do you want to make the best of your career, your education, your social life and your personal development? Surely, this can be said for everyone. Better still, how about being able to do it better with less effort? Could anyone put their hand on their heart and say they don't want this? Is it possible? Most decidedly yes, using memory techniques.

BENEFITING PROFESSIONALLY

Have you ever felt that your employer is not interested in you as a person? Have you felt there is a wide gulf between you – an *us and them* situation?

Do you want to be noticed by your employers as deserving of promotion? Do you want to be seen as someone who is gong places in the business? Yes? Then get clued up. The higher up the ranks you go the more information-based the job will be. Can any employer really afford not to look after an employee who is highly clued up on knowledge relevant to the business? Relevant knowledge is promotion currency. Those above you will be aware that if they do not advance your career others will. Furthermore, the more knowledge you have, the more effective a manager you can be. So demonstrate your knowledge of facts. Memory techniques will enable you to accelerate the acquisition of information.

Remembering facts and figures will not only impress, but it will make you a more effective manager, problem solver, *etc*. Being able to remember names pays dividends to ambitious career people in more ways than one. Which employer would you most be prepared to give your loyalty to, all things being equal – one who refers to you as 'that man', 'laddie', 'miss' or 'love', or one who addresses you by your proper name? Everybody likes to be called by their own name; it reinforces their identity. It is said that Napoleon knew the names of every one of his soldiers.

Benefits for those with ambition

Managers
Remembering names has obvious benefits for managers. Remembering the names of employees and colleagues will impress both those higher up and those below you. To those higher up it will show you are in touch with the workforce. To the workers themselves, remembering their names will communicate goodwill. It shows them they are not just units of labour. Hertzberg's theory of motivation at work suggests that quality of work is influenced by good industrial relations. Being able to remember the names of all your employees will pay dividends in terms of productivity.

Sales people
Have you noticed how highly trained sales people tend to ask you your name early and use it time and again throughout the negotiations? It's not unpleasant, is it? In fact, it's rather flattering. The most successful sales organisations know people like the sound of their own name and they train their staff to remember them.

Addressing a complaining customer by his or her name can take the sting out of an exchange of cross words. It shows the customer that you see them not simply as another dissatisfied customer but as a unique individual with a personal grievance which you are concerned to put right.

Personnel staff
Personnel staff are likely to put people they are interviewing or training more at ease if they use their names. This will get the best out of them.

Human beings have a basic need for what we call 'social stroking'. This means being acknowledged, being assured you are important. Hearing somebody call you by name fulfils this function and considerate behaviour is likely to attract considerate behaviour in return.

EXCELLING EDUCATIONALLY

Do you want to achieve a brilliant result in your course? Doesn't everybody? Do you find exam revision boring? You're not alone; most people do. If only you could find a way of getting the same results with less effort or, better still, better results with less effort. Well, you can. Exam revision lends itself well to memory techniques.

While exam revision is boring, effectiveness is vital. Consequently, it brings its own tensions, which themselves get in the way of effective memorising.

With the aid of memory skills you can gain very high levels of storage with minimal effort. Thus, exam revision becomes less stressful. Furthermore, the use of memory techniques introduces a new element into the work. It therefore ceases to be a matter of simply going over old ground. It becomes less boring and even more interesting.

Courses with a high fact-intensity

Some courses are more fact-intensive than others: law, for example. Where this is the case, it places a high demand on memory and memory techniques can make a great deal of difference to your results.

With a bit of memory training, however, this need not be the burden it at first seems. One hundred per cent recall is really within your grasp.

Avoiding mental blocks

Have you experienced mental blocks in exams? Do you want to avoid them in future?

It's one thing to commit something to memory, but quite another to get it out again. Storage and recall are not the same things. Different skills and abilities apply. Recall is sometimes blocked by things like tension, anxiety or preoccupations. When this is so we will need cues to jog our memory, or procedures to ease our tension.

Furthermore, you may test yourself ten minutes after learning the material and satisfy yourself that you have stored it well. That doesn't mean you will be able to recall it the following day or week. It is important to know how to strengthen the knowledge taken in and make it accessible when you need it.

There are various techniques to suit different kinds of information. What is best for one thing will not be best for another. What works for names will not be the best method of remembering a process. Some methods are more time consuming than others. While they may be necessary for some kinds of memory tasks, there may be less time consuming and more effective methods for others.

BEING ACCEPTED SOCIALLY

To be accepted socially is a basic human need. Some people are satisfied with social relationships among people of their own kind, but others have a desire for social mobility.

Remembering names

Names are something people so often forget. Remembering them impresses – especially after some time. One of the greatest writers on the subject was Dale Carnegie. In *How to Win Friends and Influence People*, remembering names is given a great deal of importance. Have you ever been taken aback when someone you met once, sometime previously, has actually remembered your name? You must have made an impact. You suddenly feel important and socially effective. Everyone likes to hear their own name – it makes them feel good and validated. We tend to make friends of people who make us feel good.

It is also useful to remember telephone numbers when given them. Most people forget 99 per cent of those they are given.

Winning acceptance

People tend to aspire to acceptance in higher social circles than their own, just as they aspire to living in better neighbourhoods. The higher the social circle, the more educated and cultured people are expected to be. Acceptance will only be gained if you can demonstrate that you are cultured and educated enough to fit in. You are not likely to be accepted if you cannot. Furthermore, there are particular preoccupations which distinguish particular groups – cricket, golf, matters of morality, or social and political causes, for example. The more you can absorb, retain and recall about these subjects the more ready your acceptance will be. Moreover, the more information you have of the type which preoccupies the group the more you will sought out for conversation.

Minding your Ps and Qs

To achieve social mobility you will also need to memorise social etiquette. If you don't know the manners you will stand out a mile as not belonging.

The more cultured the members are, the more attention is paid to etiquette – manners – what is done and what is not. Picking up cutlery in the wrong order at a dinner, for example, would be quickly spotted and the offender branded as someone who does not belong. It is one thing to know the correct order of cutlery and other accepted practices for particular occasions, but you have to remember it at the time, without fumbling or hesitation. Using memory techniques can put all this information at your fingertips and, thus, smooth your path to social advancement.

DEVELOPING PERSONALLY

Economics of cognitive organisation
Descartes saw the effective use of memory as very important to cognitive efficiency. In *Rules for the Direction of Mind*, he argued if we can use it more effectively perhaps we can 'relieve the memory, diminish the sluggishness of our thinking and definitely enlarge our mental capacity'.

Remembering personal things
Here are some of the memory tasks we all have:

- names
- facts
- appointments
- likes and dislikes
- important events
- promises
- routines for things
- tasks
- areas of expertise
- people's mannerisms.

Would you like to have a significant advantage when playing cards? Well, you can have.

Many card games depend on memory and techniques can be immensely useful. Indeed, so much so that if a casino's staff suspects a player is using memory techniques they ask them to leave. This is not unofficial – it is common knowledge.

Winning in quizzes
Are you a regular contestant in pub quizzes? How about boosting your chances of winning? How about moving from winning occasionally to winning always? Learning memory techniques could make this difference.

Quizzes are becoming very popular these days. Your ambition may be to enter the highly lucrative TV quizzes and come home with the fabulous prizes they offer. If so, you will need to develop your knowledge for the audition even before the actual quiz. For such a feat you will certainly need to use effective storage and retrieval methods, such as are discussed later in this book.

It is not only quiz contestants who mug up on facts – most people like to have a good general knowledge. It makes them more interesting and effective and enables them to make sense of the world. Memory techniques can make things much easier for these people too.

Going public

Would you like to be a popular entertainer? Would you like to impress people at parties, or do shows for money? Memory feats can leave audiences stunned and lead to bookings for shows, especially in holiday resorts.

There are people who spend their time memorising very large numbers. The *Guinness Book of Records* hosts a record for *pi* memory. This is the number of places to which a person can recall the *pi* constant. Tom Morton, for example, is intending to set a record of 20,100 digits, to replace the old record of 20,013. Many people ask: 'why do people want to do things like this?' Well, look at it this way. The only difference between this and the world weight-lifting record or long jump record is that one is physical and the other is mental. They are both about the pursuit of excellence and testing of the limits of human potential.

Techniques are essential to such pursuits. If you wish to participate in this kind of sport, you will need to learn the appropriate techniques.

Memory and age

Memory declines with age, but remember, you can use enhancement techniques to offset this effect. They may even improve your ability to retain and recall things as you grow older.

SUMMARY

- Enhancing your memory can give you an edge in your career.

- An enhanced memory can make you a more successful scholar.

- Being able to remember names and things about people will make you more socially successful.

- There are many ways in which an enhanced memory can aid your personal development.

- An enhanced memory can enable you to achieve more with less effort.

DISCUSSION POINTS

1. How could an improved memory help you? Consid - all the ways.

2. Are there areas where you memory fails you particu

3. In what ways would you most like to improve your and why?

4. Have you ever been stuck for something to say at a par dinner?

2
What Do We Know About Memory?

HOW MUCH CAN IT HOLD?

Human beings have about a trillion brain cells. Memories are stored as connections between these. We have so many possible connections that the number, if written, would be about 10.5 million kilometres long. There is, therefore, plenty of room to store absolutely everything we can pack into it in a lifetime.

WHAT ASPECTS OF MEMORY ARE THERE?

Four basic components of memory can be identified:

1.   Senses.
2.   Short-term (or working) memory.
3.   Long-term memory.
4.   Central processing.

Long and short-term memory
Short-term, or working, memory lasts for only a short time – between 18 and 30 seconds. Long-term memory, however, can last for a lifetime.

Functions of memory
Memory can also be analysed into different functions. Here are a few. The list is not exhaustive:

- memory for events
- memory for knowledge
- memory for intentions
- memory for actions.

Intentional and incidental memory

In addition, we can distinguish between intentional memory and incidental memory. Intentional memory is that which we deliberately have committed to memory. Incidental memory is that which we have not.

When we intentionally memorise something we are more likely to be able to recall it than if we incidentally memorise it. Different kinds of memories are stored in different sides of the brain. Memories of processes are stored in the left hemisphere, while memories of concepts and shapes are stored in the right.

HOW DOES MEMORY WORK?

There are various ways of analysing our memory system.

The physiology of memory

Knowledge seems to be fragmented and stored in various parts of the brain, like computer data on a floppy, or hard disk. It is known that a part of the brain called the hippocampus plays a crucial role in this process. If part of the brain becomes damaged we don't therefore, lose it all. We can reconstruct the memory from what we have left.

Autobiographical memory

Indeed, it is believed that all autobiographical memory is reconstruction. Some of it we find in our heads, but the details we build up from clues. These can include:

- what we would expect to be the case
- bits of films we have seen
- books we have read
- conversations we have had.

Now I said earlier that evidence indicates that what goes into long-term memory remains there forever. Here, I have said that it is believed that all autobiographical memory is a reconstruction, a meshing together of bits we remember and bits from external sources to patch the gaps. However, these two positions are not necessarily inconsistent. Just because we cannot recall every detail and have to rely on information from other sources to fill the gaps, it does not mean we have not stored every detail. Storing and retrieval are different processes. The neuro-surgeon, Penfield, who produced evidence suggesting that nothing is ever lost, bypassed the normal recall process. He made patients relive past experiences by stimulating individual groups of neurones. This was by no means normal recall. Such manipulation bypassed the kinds of things which might normally block recall, such as interference and repression.

The cognitive perspective

The cognitive perspective on memory focuses on the processes rather than the physiology of it.

Two process theory

One of the major theories of the memory process is the two process theory. These two processes are known as short-term memory and long-term memory. Short-term memory lasts for only 18 to 30 seconds. If we do something with the information, *eg* think about it, analyse it, criticise it, *etc*, it passes into long term memory. There it remains, as some evidence suggests, for ever. Short-term memory can be enhanced by **chunking** and long-term memory by **association** (see Chapters 6 and 7).

Level of processing theory

The level of processing model suggests that there is only one memory facility. It is the degree of processing you do which determines whether you retain the material. If you don't do something with it the trace just decays and you lose the information. If you rhyme the information with something you root it to some degree. If you compare it with something, you root it a bit deeper. If you analyse, or criticise it significantly, you fix it in your head deeper still.

Modular memory theory

Modular memory theory suggests that we do not have one memory system but several. Indeed, memory itself is an extension of other cognitive abilities.

We need not be concerned with the relative merits of these theories here. Whichever is favoured will not affect the applicability of the teachings of this book. They represent different levels of analysis.

Relationship between memory and intelligence

There appear to be individual differences among people in respect of memory quality. Like intelligence, it has been attributed to differences in neural speed, though the findings are not conclusive. Contrary to what you might expect memory is not strongly related to intelligence. Recent research by myself and others at London University (Wilding, Valentine, Marshall and Cooke, 1997) lends support to this. Moreover, the results showed that natural, untrained memory does not even correlate very highly with achievement. Indeed, natural memory appears to account for only four per cent of the variance between different levels of achievement. IQ, on the other hand, accounts for 25 per cent of it. That is natural, untrained, memory. Trained memory is a different matter. Using memory techniques, there is no reason why people of average ability cannot achieve 100 per cent recall. A trained memory could enable a scholar to achieve much more highly than a person with a much higher IQ, but without a trained memory.

One of the principal authorities on memory research has argued that superior memory performance can only come about through memory training (Ericsson, 1988). This is the aim of this book – to bring about superior memory performance through memory training. As I said in *How to Study and Learn* (in this series), you can't change what you were born with, despite what some memory textbooks claim. You can, however, do a lot to sharpen up your other mental powers. This can more than compensate for any deficiency of natural memory.

Storing, retaining and recalling are different processes. Processing information can ensure that you store it well, but that doesn't mean you will ever be able to recall it.

Blocks that hinder recall

Retroactive interference
We forget things for various reasons. Retroactive interference is one such reason. Retroactive interference is where previously stored knowledge gets in the way and prevents you actually recalling information you want.

Pro-active interference
Pro-active interference is where information stored since the storage of the knowledge you wish to recall gets in the way and distorts it.

Repression
Sometimes knowledge is hurtful, or threatening to our psychological well-being. If so, we often block it. This stops it coming to the surface. According to psychoanalysts, however, repressed knowledge causes problems of other kinds.

Psychoanalytical view
Psychoanalysis is more interested in forgetting than remembering. Practitioners of this sub-discipline see forgetting as a symptom of neurosis. We tend to suppress things we do not like to think about and actually repress things which threaten the integrity of our egos. Repression means totally denying to ourselves the existence of the memory.

THE WAYS MEMORY CAN FAIL

There are a number of ways in which memories can fail. They are:

- failure in registration
- failure in retention
- failure in retrieval.

Attention
Attention is an important part of the memory system. There are two types:

- general level of attention
- distribution of attention.

Attention can be affected by:

- the level of intention to attend to something
- the kind of information
- extraneous influences.

We can, to some degree, train ourselves to improve our concentration levels and also to notice detail.

Categories of extraneous influences
The extraneous influences which affect our memory can be any of the following:

- aspects of the physical environment
- aspects of the social environment
- limitations on mental ability
- physiological condition
- mental condition.

Attitudes

Our ability to remember depends on our attitude towards the material concerned. If it is favourable and we are interested in the material we are more likely to remember it.

Emotions

Emotions significantly affect our ability to remember things. If the material arouses strong negative emotions it will be easy to recall. However, if it arouses only moderately negative emotions it will have the reverse effect. This is because moderately negative emotions cause us to suppress the material.

Sometimes we go further than suppressing it. If something threatens our psychological well-being, *ie* our ego integrity, our minds will tend to repress it. Repression is a much deeper concealment than suppression. Suppressed memories can be recalled, but repressed memories are buried so deep that we are not even consciously aware that they exist.

What is meant by threatening the integrity of the ego is that it threatens that balance we maintain in the parts of our psychological selves. This includes our self-concept of ability, our conception of how others see us, our moral and other values and our centralised beliefs. These are all things which add up to a stable balance in our personality, a balance which must not be disturbed.

Psychoanalysts believe, however, that repressed memories cause problems of their own, as they fester beneath the surface. The effects are expressed in terms of various kinds of neuroses. Unlocking these memories and bringing them to the surface can relieve a person of symptoms that damage their quality of life, such as: phobias, hysteria, obsessions or psychosomatic illnesses like psoriasis, eczema, asthma and a whole host of other physiological conditions.

Because people are not consciously aware of repressed emotions, special techniques are necessary to bring them to the surface. These include hypnotism and free association. The latter involves watching for mental blocks when a person allows their mind to produce a progressive stream of associations. The points at which the mental blocks occur are explored to see why the mind's recall became resistant at that point.

Self distortions

Sometimes, to protect our self-concept and self-esteem, we distort our memories rather than completely repress the material.

Preparing to recall material which arouses moderately negative emotions

If you want to remember material which you know is going to arouse moderately negative emotions, for example handling a dispute, you will need to enhance your ability to remember the details. An example might be writing down the key points as the dispute progresses or taping the conversation (with all parties' permission, of course). Another example would be to run over the details in our mind, or in conversation with a colleague, immediately after the meeting.

TESTING MEMORY

There are various ways of testing memory quality.

Whechsler Memory Scale

The Whechsler Scale provides a battery of tests which can give quite reliable measurements of memory quality. It contains the following six tests:

- recall of current events
- list of digits
- words
- word pairs
- short story
- geometric pattern.

These can be affected by test anxiety and guessing biases.

Self reports

Memory quality is sometimes assessed by asking people to fill in a questionnaire on their ability to remember various kinds of information. There are problems with this kind of test, of course. Many people like to think they have a good memory, for ego defensive reasons. That doesn't mean they actually have. Furthermore, what they think is a good memory might be very different to what others think.

Memory diaries

Another possibility of testing memory is to keep a memory diary. In this you would record, on a daily basis, the types of information you forget.

Testing for technique usage

Can we test trained and untrained aspects of memory? In a recent attempt to screen out a sample of people with naturally superior memories colleagues and I from the University of London needed to identify when people were using memory techniques. Otherwise, what would appear as naturally superior memories may, in fact, have been the effect of techniques. Anyone can develop these and produce superior performance. They have nothing to do with naturally superior memory.

Two tests were given for each type of memory ability. One of them lent itself reasonably well to the use of memory techniques while the other did not. For example, two tests of memory for verbal material were given. One such test was a list of words given verbally to participants. The other was a story read. The story test lends itself better to memory techniques. The results of one test were deducted from the results of the other to give the score for the effect of technique usage.

WHAT IS GOOD FOR MEMORY?

It is said that certain chemicals are beneficial to memory. These include Vitamin B, especially B1, B6 and B12. Also beneficial is folic acid, tyrosine, iodine, manganese and choline. Glucose is involved in the chemical process of storing memories and, therefore, it may be beneficial to take after study, or exam revision.

You will be able to remember things better if you get enough sleep. For this reason late nights and study do not go well together.

Alcohol has a negative effect on brain function and thus will affect your ability to store material.

As you would expect, you will not be able to store or recall memories so well when you are physically ill as when you are in the best of health.

Many drugs have a bad effect on memory and tobacco is one of them.

Emotional disturbance affects mental processing including memory. Depression actually affects the right hemisphere more than the left. You would, therefore, expect memory for spatial material to be harder to recall rather than memory for verbal material.

As has been said, attention is an important part of the memory process. If you are too comfortable attention is not as its best. Some slight discomfort or anxiety helps, though it should not be too great.

Stress has a bad effect on memory. A lot can be done to relieve this and, thus, remove its effect on your memory when you particularly need to store things, *eg* during study or exam revision. Progressive muscle clenching and release, starting at the feet and working up to the head is a good way of relaxing and relieving stress. Many yoga positions are beneficial for this purpose. Transcendental meditation and positive imaging (focusing on relaxing situations) can also help.

Don't be the absent minded professor

If you develop a reputation for having a bad memory you will indeed have one. Give a dog a bad name and it will be a bad dog. We live up to other people's expectations of us. Indeed, such expectations are one of the main determinants of our behaviour.

THE SERIAL REPRODUCTION EFFECT

Research shows that the majority of what people remember from an experience comes from the beginning and end. The material concerned may be a list of words, a story, a film, or anything else. The material they retain and recall from the first part of a list is known as the **primacy** effect. The higher level of storage achieved here is due to the fact that some degree of processing went on when the mind was not already cluttered. Material that is easily recallable from the end part of an experience is due more to there having been less time for the trace to decay (the **recency** effect). The bit in the middle suffers from insufficient capacity to process the information deeply because of the channel overload from earlier parts of the material. It has also been subjected to a longer time lapse than the material from the end of the experience. Consequently, it has been subject to significant memory decay. In addition, it has been subject to what is known as pro-active interference. This is the distorting effect of information heard, or seen subsequently, *ie* information from the end of the series.

NATURAL RHYTHM

Our ability to store and retain information is affected by natural rhythms, known as **biorhythms**. The circadian rhythm affects us all, but not in the same way. Everyone's energy level is at is lowest very early in the morning and rises gradually towards a peak. While some may peak about midday, others may rise more slowly and not peak until late in the afternoon or early evening. At your peaks you are capable of your highest level of mental performance. In your troughs you are at your lowest in this respect.

It is a myth that each hour in the morning is worth more than each hour in the afternoon. Unquestioning adherence to this principle can result in lower productivity. This, in turn, can lower self-esteem and self-concept of ability, causing students who naturally peak later in the day to underrate their true potential.

Understanding your own natural rhythm

It is important to know your own daily rhythm. This doesn't mean just how easily you get up in the morning. That has as much – if not more – to do with your evening social habits, which may fit your circadian rhythm no better than your working pattern. You can check your circardian rhythm objectively and reliably using a thermometer, as your energy level is associated with your temperature level.

Make a chart marked with the times of the day, in hours, along the bottom. Mark temperature, in degrees, on the vertical axis. Take your temperature orally an hour after getting up, then at three-hourly intervals during the day. Take a final reading just before you go to bed. Plot the readings on the chart and join them up.

Repeat the process for a week, carefully plotting the readings on the same chart. Don't expect the lines to match exactly, it is general shape that is important. At the end of a week you should be able to see clearly where your natural peaks and troughs are, in other words your circadian rhythm. Plan things according to this rather than to a rhythm which someone else tries to tell you is right. It may be right for them, but only this test will tell you if it's right for you.

Some people have more flexible body clocks than others, but to continuously fight against your own natural rhythms is counter productive.

Female cycles

The female menstrual cycle can have a severe emotional effect on some women. This pre-menstrual tension (PMT) can cause depression. This in turn affects the functioning of the right side of the brain on which spatial skills like mathematics mostly depend. The left side of the brain – used mostly in language and sequential processing – is not affected.

Women who suffer particularly badly from PMT might try scheduling revision of linguistic material for the part of the month when they suffer most, and keep the unaffected times for material of a spatial kind, such as mathematics, science or fine art.

Environmental cycles

Our bodies are also influenced by cycles in our environment. Light, and so length of day, determines the secretion of the sleep-inducing hormone melatonin. For some people, the effect is so severe that it causes a cyclical kind of depression (seasonal affective disorder, or SAD) in the winter months.

It is said that the time of the week when memory is most receptive is on a Friday and/or Saturday. This may be because of the partial attention vacuum that results from being away from work. It may also be due to a relatively relaxed state which follows the end of the working week.

It is often said that it is best to study late at night because your subconscious will then work on the material during the night. This is a plausible piece of advice because of the fact that the material stored will not become subject to pro-active interference. Pro-active interference is distortion caused by information taken in immediately afterwards. If you go to sleep immediately afterwards your waking mind takes in no further information for about eight hours, although it is reasonable to consider that dreams may have a similar effect. However, dreams do not occur during the first stages of sleep.

What are not to be taken seriously are the claims of companies who sell language learning tapes for playing whilst you're asleep. These will actually have the effect of interfering with your sleep patterns and so, overall, would have a negative effect on mental processing and learning generally.

CHOOSING THE RIGHT TECHNIQUE

Practical common-sense

Do you use any memory aids at present? Most people do. Often, these are based on practical common-sense. An example is making notes in a diary or a notebook. Putting things out of place to jog your memory that you wanted to remember something is another way. You can wear your watch on the wrong hand, or put a rubber band on your wrist for the same reason. Keeping a noticeboard in the kitchen for things to do is a good idea. Strategically placed notes can be useful too, *eg* placed where you are bound to encounter them.

What most people do

Most people tend to put things in the same place every time – 'a place for everything and everything in its place', as the saying goes.

Rehearsal

What do you do when you are given directions to somewhere? Do you write them down, or keep them in your head? Few people tend to write them down. Usually, they keep them in their head, because they are in the driving seat of a car and it would be inconvenient to write directions down. Instead, they tend to run over them in their mind. Is that what you do?

Routines

Do you have set routines? Do you do things in a particular order? Those of us who are highly organised use routines. Examples of routines include placing all incoming letters in order for replies. The first received is the first to be replied to. The last received is answered last. Checking your e-mail at the start of every day is another example. Yet another is running through a list of things you should have in your pockets before you leave for work, *eg* car keys, credit cards, diary, pen.

Why do routines work? They amount to habits formed by conditioning. They largely bypass the mental processes. It's just like the way a dog comes to expects its walk at a particular time of every day and your stomach tells you are hungry at the time you usually have your dinner. Largely bypassing the mental processes these habitual solutions free up memory and intellect for use in other tasks.

Being more organised

Do you feel you could be more organised generally in your life? Many people with good brains defeat themselves through lack of organisation. Think of the absent minded professor example. The best way is to use a diary, a personal or electronic organiser or a computer organising program.

More advanced mnemonics

An ability to remember and recall things well can improve your effectiveness in everything many-fold. Would you like to have this ability? If so, it's worth spending a little time to learn some mnemonic techniques. There are different methods to suit different needs and they all have their advantages and disadvantages. These will be explained in detail later.

SUMMARY

- There's room in our memories for more than we'll ever get time to store in them.

- We can distinguish between intentional and incidental memory.

- There is little relationship between memory and intelligence.

- Enhanced memory can improve performance many-fold.

- Memory can fail in registration, retention or retrieval.

- There are several reasons why we may forget things.

- There are various methods for testing memory quality.

- People tend to remember things from the beginning and end of an experience and often they forget things from the middle.

DISCUSSION POINTS

1. How much can you remember from your childhood?

2. What is your earliest memory?

3. Do you tend to remember trivia?

4. Are there some things you can remember better than others?

5. Are there some things you tend to forget more than others?

6. Which physical memory aids do you tend to use?

3
Putting the Material In

BEING SELECTIVE AND ORDERLY

It is estimated that 75 per cent of our communication content is redundant. That includes speech in books and papers. Consequently, we can cut down what we seek to take in by 75 per cent without losing important material if we are careful. There is no point in filling our heads with rubbish.

If you store information in a notebook on the first page which comes to hand and any space which is available on it, then you won't be able to find the information when you need it. If, on the other hand, you store it in a diary or Filofax in date or alphabetical order, you will be able to find it easily. Likewise, if you lay information you need in any available space on your desk you will not be able to go directly to it when you want it. If, instead, you file the information in a filing cabinet, in subject and alphabetical order, you will be able to retrieve it easily when you need it.

Chunking

Chunking is the equivalent, in memorising, of ordering things by subject, in physical terms. Examples of chunking are: classifying, use of acronyms and diagrams.

Chunking, or unitisation as it is sometimes called, is grouping ideas together according to a common theme and giving the group a name. It works by virtue of the fact that each bit of information stored carries a number of other bits of information. The process is dealt with in detail in chapter 6.

Building in memory techniques

Using studygrams
When you are writing your revision notes, chunk them. Do the same with lecture notes and coursework notes. In fact, build in chunking techniques for all the things you want to remember. One way of

building chunking into your revision notes is to get used to writing them in diagram form. Use of **studygrams**, sometimes called spidergrams, is a useful way of doing this. You place the important points in the middle of the page and then the points which relate directly to those further out from the centre linked by lines. Any points which relate to those, in turn, place even further out again, linked by lines (see Figure 1).

Classifying
Develop a predisposition to categorise or classify all things. Develop a set of standard shapes to use, *eg* a spot, dumb-bells, a triangle, for one, two and three points. Then make pictures with these.

Organising to understand
Make sure any material classifications make sense. Write them on paper first and amend, and amend again if necessary. Draw diagrams in such a way that the relationship between the parts is clearly indicated.

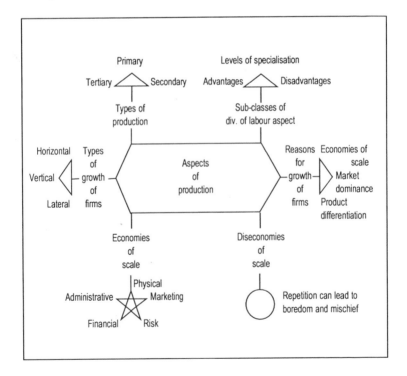

Fig. 1. A studygram for remembering aspects of production.

The *top down* method is a useful diagrammatic technique where retention of order is required. The nearer the top an item comes, the earlier in the process it occurs. If you use computer algorithm method you will find there are standard shapes for decisions, loops and case structures (for complex but programmable decisions). If the material is not clearly structured when it goes into your mind, it will be more difficult to recall than if it is clearly structured.

Analysing and synthesising
Take material you are memorising to bits and organise it so that it is meaningful to you. You have got to understand it first.

Analysing is taking the elements of knowledge to bits and categorising in different ways. Synthesising is combining the different categories in meaningful ways. An example of analysing would be to analyse a novel in terms of the characters presented, the themes, and the places. An example of synthesising might be to consider how the places have been used to reinforce themes.

Organising to commit to memory
The way we pass things from short-term memory to long-term memory is by processing them. This means doing something meaningful with them, so that the process engages with what is already in our heads. This way the new information becomes linked to that which is already there. That is how long-term memory works. If you link them intelligently and meaningfully you will be able to recall them relatively easily.

The points in the natural linking that takes place may not be the best for retrieval. After all, some of the concepts and facts the new information links to may not be directly relevant to the subject in question. However, by deliberately chunking the information purposefully, in a diagram, on paper, the links made will be more useful ones. They will link one part of the subject to another, rather than to irrelevant ideas.

Organise time to minimise interference with memorising
Suitability of study environment will vary throughout the day. For some students there will be more peace and quiet in the mid-morning or afternoon. Family members or flatmates may be constantly around in the early morning and in the evenings, rushing to get ready for school or work in the mornings – playing music or watching television in the evenings. This has to be taken into account in your plan. You need to plot time slots when you can

rely on uninterrupted peace.

University libraries are often quietest and least crowded in the evenings. City libraries are often least quiet between 4.15pm and 5.00pm when school children use them to do homework, while waiting for their parents to collect them.

There are also times of the day when certain aspects of study are not possible. Library work, for example, cannot be done after 10.00pm at most universities. College libraries tend to close around 9.00pm and town libraries often close at 5.00pm.

Methods of organising
You can organise material for memorising in many different ways:

- studygrams
- hierarchies
- mnemonics
- diagrams
- revision cards
- key points
- acronyms
- catchphrases.

Make **key ideas** bold in any form of notes, because that adds an extra dimension when memorising.

Organising in terms of key issues

When you are writing your revision notes who are you writing for? Who is going to read them? You and you alone.

When we communicate, our aim is to get our message across in as short a form a possible. Every sensible person would agree that it is pointless to write more than is necessary to achieve that aim. You will not need to write anywhere near as much to communicate something to yourself, when you are reading your notes over in the future, as you would if you had to communicate those ideas to another person. The slightest clue on paper will enable you to access whole areas of material already stored away in your mind. What on earth is the point, then, in writing all those ideas out in full? It will only lead to a waste of time in both writing and reading them, encourage a superficial treatment of the ideas (reading the matter as mere words rather than meanings), and deprive you of the chance of strengthening your memory trace by making yourself recall the material from mind.

Using keywords
Keywords and phrases are sufficient. Furthermore, long words can be shortened, for example: 'stats' for statistics. Standard abbreviations can be used, as can standard symbols, for example: ∴ for 'therefore'. You should develop your own personal shorthand. The more creative you are the easier this will be.

Marking textbooks
Another useful aid to committing material to memory is marking textbooks. Some students are reluctant to mark or highlight textbooks. But why not? What have you bought them for if not to learn? If marking them aids learning (and we know it does) then it makes sense.

Don't overdo it, though, as many do. Otherwise you will end up with so many marks that you will lose sight of what is most important. One of the things which leads to over-marking is marking as you read. Don't mark until you've read a whole section. Only then will you be able to see what the important points are.

Compiling references
Record cards are a useful medium for notes, especially if you are a research student. Ideas, together with the full biographical references, and cross references to other cards, can be stored in alphabetical order in a card-index file. Neither the cards nor the containers are expensive to buy.

Drawing pictures
Pictures are particularly useful in note-taking. There is an old Chinese saying that one picture is worth a thousand words.

Using studygrams
Another form of note-taking is the studygram or spidergram (see page 33 and Figure 1). Instead of linear form, it employs diagrammatic form. The advantage is that details of the whole subject, and all the relationships between the parts, can be viewed at once. Linear notes, on the other hand, have to be viewed in sequence.

The studygram technique relies mostly on the right hemisphere of the brain, while linear notes rely mostly on the left. It is a good idea to do your note-taking in both forms, so then you have a record in both parts of your head. Your retention and recall ability will benefit from the fact that you have had to translate the linear notes into the spatial, studygram format. Such translation strengthens the memory trace.

Reducing notes to a minimum
Another form of translation which is very useful for increasing comprehension and strengthening memory trace is successive note reduction. Reduce each section of notes to one page, then each page to one paragraph. Continue this process of reduction until you have reduced your notes for a whole subject to key points written on a single postcard. The wider information, and the way it relates to these key points, will have become rooted in your memory in this process of reduction. This activity is particularly valuable close to exams.

Note-taking involves:

- recording
- reducing
- reciting
- reflecting
- reviewing.

These are known as the 5 Rs of note-taking.

ORGANISING THE ENVIRONMENT FOR STUDYING

The way you arrange your place of study will have a good or bad effect on the progress you make. Consider such things as:

- space
- heat
- light
- freedom from noise and interruption
- comfortable seating.

Finding space
Study is a private affair. You can't memorise material while others are watching television or chatting about their holidays in the same room.

If you have a study in your house, where you can work undisturbed, in peace, you are very fortunate. For most it's the bedroom, but many children don't have sole use of that either, brothers and sisters use it too.

Adult learners
Adult learners with young children at home have particular problems here. When exams are getting close it might even be a good idea to move out for a couple of weeks and stay in a guest house or a friend's or relative's house if peace during the day and undisturbed sleep at night are unlikely.

Using a library
Where no facilities for undisturbed periods of study are available, don't try to make do with a room where other things are going on. Instead, check whether private study rooms are available at your school or college. If not, the college or town library is your next best bet. Libraries have reading tables and college libraries sometimes have private study cubicles which can be booked at the desk. At least it should be quiet in libraries and if people are making a noise you can ask the librarian to request quiet.

Adjusting heat, light and noise
Arranging your space is one thing, but for maximum efficiency other things have to be attended to as well, like heat, light and noise.

Heat
You can't memorise complex ideas if the heat is making you fall asleep. People differ as to the room temperature they prefer. But remember, you are not in the room to relax after a hard day's work, so the ideal temperature would be lower than that in which the other members of the family are watching the television. A reasonable temperature for the purpose is around 15.5°C (60°F). The type of heater used is also important. Electric fires produce their heating effect directly onto surfaces, such as the skin, without heating the surrounding air very much. Fan heaters, however, heat the air and blow it around. The effect is rather sleep inducing.

Light
Good light is important to prevent eye strain as this gives people the feeling of mental fatigue. If you feel mentally fatigued you will not be able to store material very effectively. We know that light affects our moods and levels of alertness. A reduction in the light falling on the retina starts a process of signal relays which causes the pineal gland, deep inside the brain, to secrete a hormone called melatonin. This is picked up by the hypothalamus which responds by making the body ready for sleep.

Noise

Some people say they can't study without pop music or a television in the background. This is seen by some as 'redundancy control' – the need for something to tap their excess mental energy; otherwise it is felt as anxiety. There is no evidence that pop music or any other effect selectively taps any spare mental energy. There is no reason to suppose that all mental energy can't be utilised in the memorisation process anyway. Silence is considered far better than noise for study.

There is an exception, though. It has been found by researchers in this field that some classical music, like that of Bach and Mozart, can actually enhance receptivity. This is because the beat matches the brainwave pattern that a receptive state of mind produces. This is not the case with rock music.

If silence is the most desirable it is not always achievable, whether at home, at school, or in the library. If silence is a problem, buy yourself some earplugs. They are cheap and available from most chemists.

Physical comfort

What people describe as mental fatigue is, to a large degree, muscular fatigue and much can be done to reduce it. The mind works best when there is least strain upon the body.

Two parts of the body which suffer from extended periods of study in a sitting position are the neck and the back. Avoid polyprop chairs. Their shape is designed for cheapness and rigidity, not orthopaedic comfort. Straight back chairs are best, with a high back if possible.

INTERACTING WITH EXISTING KNOWLEDGE

Raise some questions before you begin reading a text. This will make your mind work in a critical manner, making your reading active rather than passive. This will aid retention, as it amounts to processing the material and, thus, sending it into long-term memory.

Understanding long-term storage

There are two dominant theories about how long-term storage takes place. One is that we have a long and a short-term memory and processing the material causes it to pass from one to the other. The second theory is that there are no separate long-term and short-term memories, but merely one memory system only. The deeper we process the material the more it will stick. The latter makes sense when you take into account the way Piaget showed us that learning takes place. The information we take in through our sense impressions is compared with what is already there. It becomes linked and adds to the sophistication of our stored view of the world. Now we can apply enhancement to this process by deliberately recalling relevant information already in our heads.

Here is an example: Suppose you are introduced to someone whose name is John Harris. You might run through your autobiographical memory quickly to determine whether you have ever known anyone else called John Harris. Finding you have known someone with that name you might say out loud, 'Ah, I knew someone named John Harris a few years ago. He looked a bit like you too, though his hair was longer and he was a little older.' One of my favourite examples comes from an early *Dad's Army* episode. A Commanding Officer whom Captain Mainwaring had never before met recollected, on hearing his name: 'I knew a Mainwaring once. Hmm, right idiot he was.' The comparison is there, isn't it?

Remembering names

A good way of remembering names is to relate them to physical features. An example might be if you were introduced to a person called Mr Jones who was very tall and thin, you might immediately say mentally: Mr Jones has long bones. Similarly, if the person's name was Sally Crick, you might think: Sally Crick looks like a stick.

Alternatively you could relate people's names to their trade, or some other attribute. If you know a carpenter, for example, named George Wood, his name ought to be easy to remember. It's surprising, however, how we miss such connections.

Exercise
In the spaces below, write down the names of six people you know. Write in the caption space beside each box an association you might now make if you were meeting them for the first time. If it rhymes it will be even easier to recall.

Remembering faces
Remembering faces does not lend itself well to mnemonic techniques. It is socially desirable to do so, however. Everyone likes to be recognised, it makes them feel important. People hold positive attitudes towards others who recognise them and less so towards those who do not.

One technique for remembering faces is to teach yourself their anatomical structure in detail. Faces have many, many muscles, each giving its own effect on appearance. Then there is bone structure – everybody's is different. Take note of all the different kinds of skin, hair and eye colours there are. This will enhance your perception of detail.

Another thing you can do is compare people's faces with those of other people you know and note similarities and differences.

Always consciously relate what you want to remember to knowledge you already have.

Relating facts to existing knowledge
Using these two techniques you can enhance your ability to remember faces and names considerably.

When you are attempting to commit any piece of knowledge to memory ask yourself:

- Do I already know about this?
- How much of it do I already know?
- How much is new to me?
- Are there any comparisons I could make?
- Is it what I would have expected?

Criticise the knowledge. Ask:

- Do I know anything which would challenge it?
- Does it make sense?
- Are there exceptions?
- Does it hold true in all cases?
- Are there other views or explanations?
- Is the knowledge biased?
- Who is saying it and what's in it for them?

If you want to remember facts, ask:

- Do I need to know this one?
- Is it relevant?
- Is it important?
- Does it contradict what I already know?
- Is it plausible?
- Is it challengeable? If so, in what way?
- On what assumptions is it based? Are they challengeable?
- Is it useful?
- It is concise?
- Could it be reduced to make it more elegant, in the mathematical sense?
- Are there other views which contradict it?

USING MNEMONICS

To enhance your memory many-fold you can use mnemonics. The word mnemonics comes from the name of the Greek goddess of memory, Mnemosyne. Mnemonics are memory techniques for superior memory performance.

Chunking
There are two main ways we memorise things: chunking and association. Chunking is categorising material in meaningful groups (see page 33 and Chapter 6 for fuller details). Consider the following list of items:

- bread
- shampoo
- tea
- bananas
- eggs
- pork sausages

- washing powder
- bacon
- milk
- tomatoes.

From these we can extract the categories:

- breakfast foods
- washing materials
- toiletries.

Using shapes
We can use shapes to chunk material. For a start, we can employ symmetry. Suppose you have a lot of material to learn and you are able to classify it into five groups. Suppose there are five items in one group, three in two groups and two in the other two groups. A studygram which has a symmetrical shape can be formed. It would have a pentagon or pentagram (these are a five-sided figure and a five-pointed star respectively) in the middle. It would have a triangle on either side and a dumb-bells symbol above and below. Lastly, there would be a second pentagram immediately above the first. At the corners of each of these can be written the various concepts or facts concerned. The very symmetry of the studygram will make it relatively easy to remember.

Here is some information on division of labour from a GCSE Economics course. Do a studygram containing this information using the shapes in the list given in Figure 2.

Specialisation occurs at international, regional, industrial and plant levels. There are advantages and disadvantages to the division of labour. Advantages are as follows:

- Repetition of a particular task improves expertise.
- Training requirements are minimised.
- People's particular skills are fully utilised.
- Each employee will use just one piece of equipment rather than several.
- Such specialisation lends itself more to the use of machinery.

Disadvantages are:

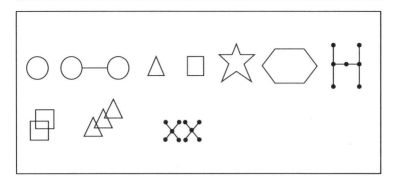

Fig. 2. Shapes useful for chunking in a studygram.

- Repetition leads to boredom and this in turn can lead to mischief.
- Craftsmanship deteriorates.
- Bottlenecks can occur.
- Employees cannot be switched from one job to another.

More advanced chunking methods are dealt with in Chapter 6. Association is covered in Chapter 7.

Using deliberate interference

When you have been storing any sequential information, for example learning a process or a poem, once you begin to feel you have mastered it complete the process by deliberately putting obstacles in your way. Make yourself recall material, or carry out a learned process, while various distractions are taking place (loud music, chatter). Put yourself into all kinds of unfavourable conditions while you apply the new knowledge to different problems or perform the new skill. Teachers used to ask pupils to say their tables backwards to complete the learning process. This is, indeed, performing the skill under unfavourable conditions.

Similarly, it will help you complete the learning of a poem, a speech, a script and many other things if you ask a friend to read a newspaper aloud while you recite the material. If you can do so under such unfavourable conditions the programming of your neural circuitry will have become quite rigidly established. Common sources of interference will, themselves, have become associated with the stored sequence, so that they do not necessarily distract you. When you can recall knowledge or carry out a skill in such distracting circumstances you will have reached a new super-height of proficiency. If you can do it when circumstances are abnormal you can be pretty sure of doing it when they're not.

SUMMARY

- Reduce information to the essentials prior to memorising.

- Organise the information meaningfully.

- Studygrams provide a useful means of organising material to be memorised.

- Algorithms are a useful means of organising material of a sequential nature.

- Organise your environment for maximum receptivity of mind.

- Make the new knowledge you are learning interact with existing knowledge.

- Combine chunking with association.

DISCUSSION POINTS

1. How much preparation do you do prior to memorising material?

2. If you are chunking, what kind of chunking do you use?

3. In what ways do you organise things prior to memorising?

4. Is there a good balance to be struck between the time you have to spend in structuring prior to memorising and simply getting on with memorising? Where do you stop in organising? Is any time you spend improving organisation of material worth the time and effort, or do you have to draw the line somewhere?

4
Keeping It There

In addition to measures for effectively storing information you can also take measures to strengthen your long-term retention of it.

TESTING REGULARLY

Regularly testing yourself on material is one way of doing this.

Serial reproduction effects

Research has shown that when we receive information over a period of time (*eg* a one hour lecture, a half hour conversation, a TV programme or by reading a chapter of a book over a 45 minute period) we tend to remember details from the first and last parts fairly well, but not from the part in the middle. This is discussed more fully on page 28. There are ways of counteracting this effect.

Testing yourself
One effective method of testing yourself and correcting for errors is as follows. When you are learning some material take a ten-minute break and do something entirely different. During this time do not think about the material you have been reading. The interval of ten minutes is chosen because this is the point of highest recall – ten minutes after encounter. Test yourself after ten minutes and correct any errors in your recall. Overlearn those corrections. Overlearning is going over them again and again, even though you appear to be recalling them correctly. Overlearning, although boring, is a means of strengthening your memory trace. Test yourself after a further 24 hours and, again, correct the errors and overlearn the weak areas. Do the same after a week and the same again after a month. By this time the material will be pretty firmly rooted in your long-term memory.

When should you test yourself?
It is useful to test yourself on material you have to use just before you are going to have to use it. This means minutes before, where

the knowledge is not complex. Examples of this kind of knowledge are algorithms, procedures and lists. You will need to test yourself hours before you will need the knowledge where it is more considerable or complex: such as exam material.

Advantages of mnemonics
An advantage of mnemonics is that you can run through material and test yourself when you have a few moments to spare. No one would reasonably suggest you go on regularly testing all your knowledge throughout your life – as you store more and more you simply would not have time to do anything else. However, in the period which leads up to an exam on a subject the effort will pay dividends.

REPROCESSING FREQUENTLY

You can keep stored knowledge alive in your head by applying the knowledge to your environment and social circumstances whenever possible.

Ask questions about the knowledge
It is useful to question knowledge you have and frequently test the limits of its applicability. Does it explain this or that situation, for example?

Hypothetical situations
Try to think of situations where knowledge you have stored would not explain things as it normally does. IQ, for example, is a good predictor of school achievement, but it ceases to be so at very high levels of the scale. Einstein's special theory of relativity explains gravity in certain circumstances, but not all. This is why he subsequently devised his general theory of relativity.

The different parts of knowledge
Knowledge consists of different parts:

- assumptions
- models
- facts
- evidence
- theories
- opinions
- beliefs

- attitudes
- values.

You can use all of these to challenge knowledge periodically.

Challenging the assumptions
All knowledge is based on assumptions and in the end these are unprovable. An example is that competition will always lead to greater efficiency and work out in the interests of the consumer. This is based on the assumption that humankind is basically selfish and this cannot be proved. In contrast, the theory that public ownership of the means of production (*ie* socialism) will bring about a fair, prosperous and stable civilisation without crime or conflict is based on the assumption that humankind is naturally social and co-operative. Nor is this provable.

One way of keeping your knowledge alive is by changing the assumptions – replacing them with alternatives, to see if the theory still holds true.

Applying different models
Models are simplified explanations of the way things work or relate to each other. They rarely exist in isolation. There are invariably different ways the same things can be explained. The two factor model of memory (long-term memory and short-term memory) and the level of processing model are examples. The former suggests there are actually two major parts to the memory and both are relatively distinct from each other. The latter suggests there is only one memory but that information can be processed at different levels. If the information stays in the memory it is not because it has passed from short-term memory to long-term memory, but that it has been processed deeply and has, therefore, taken strong roots. Try applying different models to knowledge you have stored.

Challenging the evidential basis for inferences
Another way to keep stored material alive is to challenge the evidential basis for inferences made. Evidence can be strong or weak. It can never prove anything is the case, for competing explanations might arise in the future, which could not be anticipated at present. Evidence can, however, disprove things. This is not the only way we can think about evidence, though. In law a different set of criteria applies. Judges speak of cases conclusively proved. This is because the definition they use of the

term *conclusively proved* amounts to *beyond reasonable doubt.* That is
a very different thing to saying this amounts to unshakeable proof.
   Evidence can also be analysed in the following ways:

- conclusive (in science evidence can conclusively disprove but not
  prove)
- persuasive
- suggestive.

Often evidence used in the social sciences is statistical in nature. The
limits of statistical evidence should be understood. For example,
statistical evidence is always subject to confidence levels. A very high
level of statistical confidence is known as one per cent level.
However, it must be understood, that this means there is only one
chance in 100 that the conclusion the statistics suggest could be due
to chance. But if the statistical data refers to 100 different findings it
implies that one of them will be due to chance alone.

Be open-minded
It is sensible to be consciously aware that much knowledge can only
really be held tentatively. It will always be subject to revision in the
face of fresh evidence. Far too many people believe all the
knowledge they hold is unshakeable and right for all time.

Be on the lookout for competing theories
What has been said earlier about models applies also to theories.
While models are simplified explanations of processes, or relationships between parts of something, theories go a bit further. They are
rooted in evidence. Theories are made up of two or more constructs
supported by evidence. Constructs are relationships between two
things. Therefore, a theory amounts to, at its most basic, a statement
that A is related to B and B is related to C.
   Like models, theories rarely exist in isolation; there is invariably
more than one to explain the same thing.

Looking at it from other people's viewpoints
The plausibility of knowledge depends on where you're standing. The
desirability of the capitalist system to provide the best allocation of
resources in society will seem the best option to those with most
chance of economic success in life. However, the socialist's answer
will appear the best option for those with least chance. Trying to
stand in other people's shoes when you consider the knowledge you
have stored will help you to keep that knowledge alive.

TALKING ABOUT IT

Never pass up an opportunity to talk about your stored knowledge. This way you will be reprocessing it and adding to the complexity of its roots in your mind. You are having to defend it from challenges.

Bringing knowledge to the surface and testing

Bring knowledge you are eager to retain to the surface and test yourself on it. Perhaps, from time to time, you will find gaps and have to plug them, either by seeking material from the person to whom you are speaking, or by computing, reasoning, or perhaps even guessing. If the latter, your guesswork may be tested in the conversation. Alternatively, you may create a logical and reasonable section of argument to fill.the gaps. You can also consult your notes after the conversation and make good the spaces, or amend your temporary patches, if necessary.

That does not mean boring your friends and relatives with information irrelevant to them. Anyone who is not interested will add nothing to your knowledge. However, anyone who is interested and wants to talk about it is a different matter. Opportunities for discussion will arise at social occasions – chatting or having lunch with colleagues on the same course, or with the same interests.

Sharing your knowledge
Where a friend's business is struggling, business or finance students can give friendly advice. Where a friend's child is struggling in a school subject similar to your college course, perhaps you could help. Psychology students may be able to use their knowledge to help a friend or relative's children who are underachieving.

When the conversation turns to a subject you know something about, don't be shy, get involved. Contribute to the conversation. That's what socialising is about. It will make you more accepted and you will also be using your knowledge. Don't sit out of it because you are unconfident, or doubt your knowledge. You can use 'I think ...' and 'My understanding is ...' to prevent being proved wrong. After all, social discussion is an exploration of ideas, not a lecture. Stored knowledge is no use if it is not going to be used. Stored names are stored so that you can use them – do so. Say people's names in conversation regularly. People love to hear them. Your popularity will increase and you will be reinforcing your memory of them.

THINKING ABOUT IT PERIODICALLY

There are times which lend themselves well to reflecting upon knowledge you have intentionally stored, for example educational course material.

Travelling
If you have organised your mnemonics well, you will be able to run through any knowledge you have been learning at times when there is nothing else to do:

- when waiting for a bus or train
- when travelling in a bus or train
- when you are a passenger in a car.

The mind is very receptive at such times, it craves something to do. This is why advertisers choose to stick posters in bus shelters, on the backs and sides of lorries and buses and in trains.

Quiet times
Quiet times are also useful for running over knowledge you need to remember. Here are a few examples:

- when you have a few moments to yourself
- when there is a film on television in which you are not interested
- when you are lunching alone
- when you are having a quiet drink at a pub and there is no one to talk to.

Driving
A word of warning – because of the considerable mental effort and intense concentration required, these practices are not recommended when driving. You can deflect your attention from the road conditions and fail to see dangers in time. 'Channel overload' can also result from trying to do too many taxing things at the same time. This can threaten the safety and skilfulness of your driving.

Walking
Walking is a good time to think. The action of walking briskly releases endorphins, the body's natural tranquillisers, and this results in a feeling of calm. These are good opportunities to give unbroken attention to mentally demanding reflections.

USING PHYSICAL MEMORY AIDS

There is nothing wrong with using external, physical methods to keep stored material available and recallable.

Written reminders

One of the commonest methods which people use is written reminders. Somebody once said that one should never trust to memory what can be written down. To some degree, this is true: there is no point in overloading your memory with reminders which can be written down. The problem is, however, you may not always have a pen and paper with you and papers and notebooks can, themselves, become misplaced.

Where you just want to remember details
Sometimes you just want to remember details connected with something. An example is points to remember when replying to a letter received. A handy and cheap method is to use small pads of sticky labels sold for the purpose in most stationery shops.

Where you need to be alerted in the first place
Sometimes you need to be reminded to do something. A useful device for this is to strategically pin notes on the wall, the phone or the dashboard of your car. If the reminder is for first thing in the morning, then place a note on your pillow, or in your shoes. Sometimes you will need to be alerted to do something on your way to work. A note placed on the seat of your car will do the trick.

Scheduling

Remembering things you have to do throughout your day requires organised scheduling. There are various efficient aids you can buy to help with this.

Paper-based devices
Every busy person should keep a **diary** for appointments. There is no point in placing such taxing demands on your memory system, however well you have organised it. Often people keep a large desk diary and a small pocket diary. Large desk diaries permit much greater detail than small pocket diaries. One of the problems some people find in keeping diaries is that they tend to write too much detail. Quite some time ago I made a rule for myself that I would make no notes longer than five words in any diary.

Wall charts are another option. The advantage here is that you can see the whole year at a glance. They are cheap to buy and often have public holidays shaded in to enable fast perception. In addition to writing on them with pen, various sticky symbols and labels are also available. These can be removed or swapped from place to place without unsightly crossings out, as would be the case with written material.

For the more ambitious there is the Filofax: sophisticated personal organisers that contain a diary, address book, telephone number list and various other day-to-day record books.

Electronic organisers

In today's world, more or less anything that is available on paper is available in the form of electronic pages too.

Pocket organisers are now in common use and they come in various degrees of sophistication and price. Into these you can enter the same kind of detail as you can enter into a diary or personal organiser. One of the main advantages is that you can recall material much faster. They can also provide automatic interactions between different parts of the information held in different records. In addition, a great deal more information can be stored than is the case in a paper-based organiser. Some of them can even interact with your personal computer, passing data to it and taking data from it.

There are now very useful organiser software packages for desk and notebook computers. The advantages these have over the pocket organisers is that they use a larger screen and have access to greater amounts of memory. The disadvantages are, of course, that they are not so portable.

Watches with alarms are another useful device. These can hold many settings over the course of the day and can have standard settings to activate an alarm every day, on certain days of the week only, or even at certain times of the year. Some watches can even store notes.

Voice reminders

Electronic **voice reminders** can be useful things, too. These are devices which serve the purpose of a notebook or simple diary but which can be used when it is not convenient to make written notes. When you are walking or driving important ideas may come into your head. By the time you are able to write them down, though, you may well have forgotten them. A voice reminder overcomes this problem.

When you just need detail without alert
There are a number of ways that you can physically store details besides writing them down. One of the ways is to phone a message onto your **answerphone**.

If you carry a portable **dictation machine**, you could record a message to yourself on that. The disadvantage of both of these solutions to the problem is that they can only be transcribed sequentially. You have to chug through all the other information until you get to the bit you need. However, this is not as big a problem as it might at first seem. It is one of the things you naturally do – transcribe your answerphone from start to finish. Likewise, with your dictation machine, either you or your secretary will transcribe the notes.

If you have a habit of leaving your car keys in different places it might be worth buying a beeping **key ring**. These let out an electronic beep when the owner whistles, enabling them to be located.

Another way of remembering detail is to ask a friend to remind you. The problem is that the friend may forget.

Where you need alerting at a certain time
There are a number of ways of ensuring you are alerted at a certain time. You don't have to overtax your memory. Many watches now have alarms. So do pocket organisers and mobile phones. Failing this you can set your bedside or mantelpiece clock to alert you. Alternatively, and especially if you have a habit of switching alarm clocks off as soon as they ring, you can order an alarm call from the telephone operator.

Putting things out of place
A way of reminding you that you have to remember something is to put things out of place. Examples of this include:

- wearing a rubber band around your finger, or wrist, or placing one around your keys
- tying a knot in your handkerchief
- wearing your watch on the wrong arm, or with its face down.

Things in place
It is also useful to place things where they will be expected. Here are some examples:

- pen and pad by the phone

- car keys on hall table
- umbrella in the hall stand
- TV remote control in a chair-arm holder
- wallet on dressing table
- driving documents in car file
- credit cards and bank cards in special bank card wallet
- tools in correct racks
- books in author order on the shelf.

Adopting the principle 'a place for everything and everything in its place' saves no end of stress.

SUMMARY

- Test yourself after ten minutes, one hour, one day, then one month.

- Correct your errors and overlearn each stage for maximum retention.

- Keep knowledge alive by frequently reprocessing.

- Talk about the knowledge you have memorised.

- Think about it at quiet times and waiting times.

- Use physical memory aids where convenient.

DISCUSSION POINTS

1. How often do you test your memory for exam revision material?

2. How can you find opportunities to recall things you have to memorise for exams? Think of all the possible situations you could exploit.

3. In what ways can you test your knowledge from time to time? Consider all the possible ways you could do this.

5
Getting It Out

You may store and retain information well but that does not automatically mean you will be able to recall it.

REMEMBERING THE STRUCTURE

Everything has structure and the more you analyse the structure of information, the easier it will be to remember.

As has already been pointed out, material we take in through our senses is 75 per cent redundant. That is, we can cut out 75 per cent of it and still retain the important information, providing we know which bits to cut out. This takes careful scrutiny and selection. The process pays dividends, however. It can mean that it cuts down our storage task to 25 per cent of what it would otherwise be.

As has also been pointed out earlier, it is as easy to store large chunks of information as it is to store small chunks. If you organise the material carefully in the right sort of chunks, you will be able to increase your storage rate many-fold. Furthermore you will be able to do this without relative extra effort.

Spatial structure
Did you organise the material into a spatial structure, *eg* a studygram? If you did, it should be easy to recall since our right hemisphere can deal with the whole structure at once. If, on the other hand, things have been stored as a list, it will be our left hemisphere which recalls it. This acts in a sequential way and recall will be more difficult.

Did you structure the input symmetrically?
If you made a studygram, did you try to make it symmetrical? Making a studygram symmetrical is a good way of making it memorable. A completely irregular shape is far more difficult to remember than a symmetrical shape.

Does the material have a natural structure?
You can build a structure onto which the comprehensive details of any piece of knowledge can be hung. Your task will then be to go to each part of the structure and ask yourself what should be here? Here are some of the categories of knowledge which can be applied to any subject. They can be used to build such a structure:

- facts
- dimensions
- concepts involved
- models
- theories
- laws
- evidence
- strengths and weaknesses
- paradigms
- assumptions
- utilities.

Mnemonics
Was there a mnemonic to remember the different concepts and order in the structure? It is very useful to build mnemonics into a studygram. Acronyms are particularly useful to jog your memory of the individual details in each group.

Sequential structure
Is there a sequential structure to the material? Sequential structures are more difficult to remember. However, they can be structured on paper in the form of a flow process chart or algorithm prior to storing. It is sometimes also useful to highlight bottlenecks in a process, a practice known as **critical path analysis**. The more structured the input the easier it will be to recall.

Can a natural, sequential structure be inferred?
Just as common structures can be inferred in respect of spatial material, so it is possible to do so in respect of sequential material. Here are some elements of a structure which can be applied to most knowledge areas of a sequential nature:

- concepts
- models
- lines of communication, or flow

- lines of influence
- evidence supporting
- strengths and weaknesses
- bottlenecks
- critical paths
- hierarchies
- decision points
- case structures
- loops.

GOING THROUGH THE ALPHABET

Words and names can sometimes be recalled by running through the alphabet. Did the name begin with A, B, C, D, *etc*? Similarly, you can ask did it begin with Ba, Be, Bi, Bo, Bu, or Ca, Ce, Ci, Co, Cu? This latter techniques jogs the memory best. Where it works best is in recalling:

- names
- words
- spellings.

It is known as the **tip of the tongue** technique.

Sometimes you will get the suspicion that a particular letter sounds right but you still can't recall the word. Simply move onto another letter or start adding third letters to the sound you are making, *eg* Bab, Bac, Bad, *etc*.

If the tip of the tongue technique is not quite working you can estimate the number of consonants in the word. Also, try out the rhythm sound in your mind until it sounds right. Then go back to the tip of the tongue technique. If this still doesn't work, think of vowel sounds in the word; there may be long vowels like *ou*. If this doesn't work, go back to the tip of the tongue technique and then back to the rhythm technique. Keep moving backwards and forwards between the different strategies. If none of them works have a break and try again later.

RECALLING SHAPES

Some people are better than others at storing and recalling shapes of names or words. It will help if they have not only read it but written it down. People's hemisphericity differs from person to person. Some are more left brain dominant than others. Those who are the more left brain dominant are most likely to benefit from the sounds strategies. The others are most likely to benefit from the shape strategies.

Symmetry

If the word has a tall consonant at each end, or one in the middle, or perhaps no tall letters at all, the symmetry can help you recall how to spell it. Similarly, it may have one or more double letters. Symmetry is an easy thing to spot. Take a mental note of it if it is there.

Our brains process spelling in two ways. The left hemisphere processes the spelling of words in terms of sound. The right hemisphere processes the spelling of words in terms of shape. We can use both hemispheres to help ensure that we spell things correctly.

Often people cannot confidently spell a word out loud, but can tell it is right once they have tried writing it down. Cued recall is often more helpful to us than free recall. Cued recall is when something jogs our memories – in this case the actual sight of the word on paper. If this does not work then try the word building approach, building the word from monosyllables.

Formulae

There are various ways of committing formulae to memory.

Remember the actual roles

Think of the variables involved. This is by far the best way, for it is much more important to remember the formula in terms of the variables involved than as a set of letters and signs. Symbols often reflect the actual variables involved, *eg* the term Sr, as used in statistics, stands for standard error and the O and E in the Chi Square formula stands for observed and expected values. It is much more meaningful to remember observed minus expected values than it is to remember O – E.

Where the symbols do not reflect the roles

Unfortunately, the symbols do not always reflect the concepts they stand for. For example, the statistical term r^2 is used for the Coefficient of Determination (see my book *Research Methods* in this series). This could not be jogged into recollection by its algebraic symbol. If such is the case, and you can't remember the actual concepts and rules, then try to visualise the formula. Was there any degree of symmetry in it? Consider, for example:

$$r^2 = \frac{\Sigma(\hat{v}\text{-}\bar{y})^2}{\Sigma(v\text{-}\bar{y})^2}$$

This has some rough symmetry in the bracketed parts – the one accent missing from the symmetry may, in fact, help jog it into consciousness. This will be especially so when you have actually taken notice of the symmetry in a formula on storing the material.

LOOKING FOR CUES

Is there anything at all about the number, word or concept which you can remember? If there is, this may be used as a starting point to jog your memory into recalling the rest.

Numbers
If what you are trying to recall is a number, think:

- Did you make any mathematical associations?
- Did you sum the digits?
- Was there any symmetry to the number, *eg* 256652?
- Were there any double numbers?
- Were there any interesting combinations, or groupings, such as 20 + 3 = 18 + 5 in a number 203185?

Words

Rhymes and associations
Can you hear the word? Did it seem to rhyme with anything? Did you make any associations with any other word or idea?

Names
Suggestions have already been made about how we might enhance our ability to remember names by using mnemonics. Let us assume here, however, that you have not used any memory techniques when storing a name you wish to recall. What can you do?

Origins
Were there any ethnic origin clues in the name or in the person whose name it was? Does the age of the person or the social grouping to which he or she belongs suggest any possibilities?

Associations and comparisons

Sometimes when you hear a person's name for the first time, you think of other people with the same name. Was this the case here? Did you make any other associations apart from comparisons with others holding this name? For example, were there any interesting connections between the person's name and their physical appearance, or occupation?

Shopping lists

Do you make shopping lists before you go shopping? If you do, have you ever arrived at the supermarket only to find you have lost your list, or left it behind? One way to help ensure you miss nothing important is to run through making each meal for each day for a week or month as applicable.

Alternatively, some people just walk up and down each aisle checking to see if there is anything they need from what is on show.

Losing things

Losing things is very frustrating, it wastes a lot of time. We all do it, however, from time to time.

Looking back

One way to begin trying to find the lost item is to think when you last had it and retrace your steps from there. Another way of proceeding is to think where you have found the same thing at other times in the past when it has been mislaid.

THINKING AROUND

When you are trying to remember something that occurred sometime previously, one way of proceeding is to think around the subject rather than directly on it. When we cannot recall things that ought really to be easy to recall, our mind is playing mischievous tricks on us. Something is stopping us remembering it. Something is obscuring it from our view. It may be that we don't really want to remember it, or that something negative happened around the same time. In the latter case, our minds will tend to suppress the memories associated with the negative occurrences.

Using the six analytical questions

We can structure our 'thinking around' by using the six analytical questions:

- Who?
- What?
- When?
- Where?
- How?
- Why?

Who and what?

Think who was there when the idea, word, name, or whatever else came up in conversation. Did they play any role in the discussion? Did they respond, or comment on the thing you are trying to remember? What was the general subject of discussion?

When and where?

What time of the day was it when the fact, word, name, or whatever else was raised? Was it morning, afternoon or evening? Was it a weekday or a weekend? If you think about who else was present this may give you a clue to what time of the day it was if you can't otherwise remember. Similarly, if anyone was absent, was it because they were at work? Perhaps they were away on some business they always attend to on a particular day, or particular time? Where did the discussion take place? Was there anything about your surroundings that you particularly noticed?

How?

Ask yourself how did the fact, name, word, or whatever else, arise in conversation? What were people talking about?

Why?

Ask yourself why did this topic, fact, word, or name come into the conversation?

Recall your feelings when you were discussing the issue

Try to think what your feelings were when the name, word, fact, or whatever else you are trying to remember arose last. Were you happy or sad? Were you tired or wide awake? Were you interested or bored?

All of these considerations amount to thinking around, rather than directly onto, the fact which is eluding you. In this way, you may be able to bypass any mental block your mind is placing upon the material.

RELAXING

Anxiety has a negative effect on memory. Everyone who has ever taken an important exam will have experienced, to some degree, the phenomenon of mental blocks. This is anxiety restricting ability to recall things. Consequently, a direct way of overcoming this problem is to remove the anxiety. One way of achieving this is by relaxation.

Achieving relaxation

There are techniques for relaxation and they work.

Successive body parts relaxation
Relaxation can be achieved and anxiety reduced by successively attending to different body parts working from the feet upwards. Lie in a comfortable position and screw your toes up tight. Maintain the pressure for a count of ten seconds and then relax them, breathing deeply as you do so. Next, clench your calf muscles and hold the pressure for ten seconds. Let go and breathe deeply. Next your thigh muscles should be clenched and the clench held for ten seconds. Let go, and breathe deeply. You will already be feeling the relaxation in those parts of your body. It will feel as though you have put your feet up after strenuous exercise.

Work upwards to the shoulders, attending separately to every single part of the body. From the shoulders work outwards to the hands, and then go to the neck and face. There are several muscles on the face, and this practice will involve facial contortions. By the end of the process, if you have been clenching and relaxing for even periods of ten seconds and breathing deeply in between, you will really notice the degree of relaxation you have achieved. Good breathing control will enhance the process even more and it is to this we turn next.

Breathing control
Usually we inflate our chest and contract our stomach when we breathe in, and the reverse when we breathe out. To relax, however, you have to reverse the process. You distend your stomach as you inhale and contract your chest. When you exhale you do the reverse, contract your stomach and expand your chest. Furthermore, you should try to breathe evenly and slowly. In between each of your successive muscle clenchings and relaxing, breathe like this for a count of ten slow breaths.

Exercise
Another natural way to relieve anxiety is by exercise.

There are two reasons for this. One is that it takes up the adrenaline generated by stress or anxiety. The other is that the body produces natural tranquillisers called endorphins during exercise. Jogging is one useful way of exercising the whole body. Swimming is even better.

Stroke your pet
It is known that stroking an animal is beneficial in terms of relieving stress and anxiety.

Diversions

Another way of relaxing is to turn away from the source of anxiety. During exam revision, if you're finding it difficult to recall material then have a break.

Music
Music has a calming effect on the mind, providing you choose the right type. Some music, *eg* the classical music of Bach, Haydn and Handel, has the effect of making the brain more receptive. This is because the beats match beta waves of the brain. Consequently, this will be beneficial not only in helping you to recall material, but also at times when you wish to store it as well.

LEAVING IT TO THE UNCONSCIOUS

Just because you cease to consciously think about something it doesn't mean your unconscious mind gives up on it too. Indeed, turning consciously away from a problem, such as inability to recall something, often results in a spontaneous recall several minutes later. How often have you given up on trying to remember a name and some minutes later found the name suddenly came to you?

Going to sleep

Your unconscious continues to work while you are awake, but it really comes into its own while you are asleep. It is not at all unusual for people to go to sleep contemplating a problem and wake up with an answer to it.

COMPUTING

The *Mastermind* contestants appear to perform amazing feats of memory and to have enormous stores of knowledge which they can access at will. It's not quite like that, though. What they do is quickly decide whether a question falls into one of three categories:

- the answer is known
- the answer is not known, but computable
- the answer is not known and not computable.

If it falls into the latter category they quickly move on to avoid wasting time. Many of their answers, however, fall into the second category – *not known, but computable* – from the clues available. They quickly make a calculated guess. Some of the time they're wrong, and some of the time they are right. When they are right, however, viewers tend to assume they had known the answers. They had not, they had known relevant material which helped them arrive at them. Therefore, it is an important aspect of developing a powerful memory to learn to react to all memory demands in terms of asking these three questions:

- Is it known?
- Is it computable?
- Is it not known and not computable?

Let's know consider in what ways things might be computable.

Finding words

The need to recall a word is a good example of the use of computing. Trying to find the right word is a problem often experienced by many people.

Prefixes

Is the word you are looking for likely to have a particular prefix? Remember, the prefix *a* negates the meaning of a similar, non-prefixed word. For example, the word *a*political means not political. The prefix *pre* implies before whatever the rest of the word means. For example, the word *pre*view means to view before something or other. The prefix *anti* gives the word a preventative meaning in relation to what the rest of the word means. For example, *anti*septic means preventing something becoming septic. There are many more of these.

Word length and shape
Depending on your hemisphericity balance (the degree to which the left hemisphere of the brain is dominant over the right hemisphere) you may be able to visualise what the word looks like. Those who are least left brain dominant will be more inclined to be able to visualise words, because their right hemisphere, which deals with spatial processing, has a greater role in their information processing.

Common roots
Many words in the English language have common roots. If you know other words which mean similar things to the meaning you have in mind, think of their roots and this may help you compute the word you require.

RECONSTRUCTING

Much of what we interpret as memories of past events is actually reconstruction. It is generally held now that we remember bits of the past and we simply fill in the gaps from the many sources available. These include memories from dreams (daydreams and night dreams), conversations, films, stories and so on. If we know that some of what we recall of the past is simply reconstruction, then perhaps we should consciously apply ourselves to the reconstruction process rather than simply trying to recall every fine detail.

Consulting sources
If we want to remember things from the past, then instead of trying to squeeze out what seem like stubbornly unyielding bits of information from our memories, then perhaps we should go directly to more reliable sources.

Diaries and notepads are examples of such sources. If you keep diaries, you will have a pretty reliable source of facts of past events. If you don't keep diaries then perhaps somebody else has some and you may be able to obtain the information you require from them.

Newspapers are another source. These might fill in some of the gaps in the memories you are trying to recall.

If you remember who else was there at the time, why not consult them? This makes a lot of sense because the gaps that have occurred in their recollections of events might not be the same gaps that have occurred in yours. Similarly, the fragments which they managed to recall may well be different fragments from yours. This is, indeed, making good use of memory, for you are utilising the collective memory of more than one person.

Dictionaries
If you are trying to remember a word, or the spelling of a word, without much success, why bother? Go straight to a dictionary. This, too, is good use of memory, for a dictionary is an externalised memory compiled for the purpose. Clutter the mind with things you do not need and it will work sluggishly.

Other reference books
The same can be said of other reference books. These, too, amount to externalised memory.

Piece together what you have
To complete the reconstruction process you have to piece together what you have. You have to connect up the bits you held in your head with the bits you have had to find from other sources.

Patch the gaps
You may still find you have gaps. There may have to be some guesswork involved in filling these. What is guessed must be consistent with what is not and provide a reasonable completion of the picture, formula, or whatever else is concerned.

It's the natural way
It may seem that this is all a bit hit and miss. However, although most people don't realise it, it's the way we naturally recall past events. By being consciously aware of this and consulting reliable sources your reconstructions may be more accurate than they would otherwise be.

It has to fit
Where formulae are concerned, you will know if what you have patched with is right. If it is not, the formulae won't work.

SUMMARY

- Try to remember the structure.

- Use the tip of the tongue technique for words.

- Try to remember the shape.

- Was there symmetry?

- Look for any cues.

- Where words are concerned, ask how many syllables did they have and what did they start with?

- Think around the subject rather than directly on it if the recall is stubbornly unyielding.

- Recall your feelings at the time and who was around.

- Use relaxation techniques.

- Try to compute the material.

- Utilise the unconscious.

- Consult sources, such as dictionaries and reference books, to help jog your memory.

6
Chunking

We have dealt so far with rather general and common-sense ways of enhancing your ability to store, retain and recall things. The remainder of this book deals with more serious memory training techniques.

WHAT IS CHUNKING?

Centuries ago, John Locke, in *Essay concerning human understanding*, realised the value of chunking. He called it **unitisation**. He listed three rules for the process:

- choose a number of specific ideas
- give them a connection and make them into a single idea
- tie them together with a name.

Consider the following list:

- bread
- shampoo
- tea
- bananas
- eggs
- pork
- washing powder
- bacon
- wine
- tomatoes.

This could be chunked as follows:

- foods
- drinks
- household cleaning items.

USING ACRONYMS

Acronyms are very useful for chunking. To make an acronym you take the initial letters of a number of ideas and make a word out of them. Suppose you wanted to remember the names of a group of actors in a play. Suppose they were:

- Peter
- Lionel
- Andrew
- Yvonne
- Elizabeth
- Ruth
- Susan.

Taking the first letter of each name we make the acronym *players*. It would be difficult to remember the list as it was originally. It would be easy, however, to remember the word and work out what each letter stands for.

You may be able to recall a list of 11 names reasonably easily by making two words out of the initial letters, for the males and another for the females. Consider the following:

- Billy
- Roger
- Edward
- Andrew
- Donald
- Barbara
- Ursula
- Tracy
- Tanya
- Elizabeth
- Rachel.

The first letters of these names make up the words bread and butter (not the *and*, of course). This would be easy to remember. The letters of each word may be enough to trigger the recall of each person's name. Using this technique you will certainly have a much better chance of remembering the names than without it, for human beings are rather poor at remembering lists longer than seven items.

With a little squashing into shape, using extra vowels, acronyms can be made of most groups of words or names.

Be imaginative
Sometimes you have to rearrange the letters in order to make a meaningful word. If you have to do this you lose the retention of order of ideas, or facts. If you have to retain the order there are better techniques to use.

Sometimes, even rearranging the initial letters will not be sufficient to form a meaningful acronym. You may have to use the initial pairs of letters instead. These will usually contain a vowel and a consonant. If even this fails then use the first three letters. With a little imagination useful acronyms can invariably be made.

Large chunks are as easy to remember as small chunks
The size of units does not affect our ability to remember the ideas. For example, long acronyms are as easy to remember as short ones, and yet they contain more letters and, therefore, represent more ideas. Consequently, it is better to chunk things into a few large chunks, for example large acronyms or catchphrases than it is to chunk them into lots and lots of small groups.

USING CATCHPHRASES

Catchphrases are phrases wherein the first letter of each word represents the initial letter of a fact or concept. The intention is to jog the memory enough to recall the fact or concept concerned. An example is a catchphrase which I recommend for school children to remember the concepts and order of variables in the three trigonometrical ratios:

$$\text{sine} \quad = \frac{\text{opposite side}}{\text{hypotenuse}}$$

$$\text{cosine} \quad = \frac{\text{adjacent side}}{\text{hypotenuse}}$$

$$\text{tangent} \quad = \frac{\text{opposite side}}{\text{adjacent side}}$$

This can be remembered by the catchphrase:

Some of Harry's cars are having trouble on acceleration.

Here is an exercise to give you a chance to try this out for yourself.

Make up a catchphrase to remember the ingredients of leek soup. They are:

Leeks   ....

Potatoes   ....

Butter   ....

Water   ....

Milk   ....

Pepper   ....

Cream   ....

Egg yolk   ....

Place the words of your catchphrase on the line next to each word. Close the book and go and do something else, make a cup of tea, have a sandwich, read the paper or chat to somebody. After ten minutes test yourself to see if you remember the ingredients.

The first to spring to mind are often the best
As with all mnemonics, the first catchphrases to spring to mind are often the best. If you chop and change much your recall of your catchphrases or other mnemonics may be distorted by retro-active interference. Retro-active interference is the distorting effect of material stored prior to the material in question.

Exploiting the absurd
People tend to remember the absurd particularly well. Therefore, try to exploit this quality in forming your catchphrases. It also makes them more memorable if you exaggerate their qualities.

Advantages
Catchphrases are quicker to formulate than acronyms.

USING SHAPES

Having a standard list of shapes to represent numbers of items from one to ten is a useful way of quickly devising memorable studygrams.

A set of shapes for making memorable studygrams was given in

Figure 2 on page 45.

Group your memory sensibly according to themes: for example, theories, parts of a process, advantages and disadvantages. Choose for each group a shape which has the same number of corners as there are items in the group. Quantities of 1 and 2 are, of course, exceptions. Arrange the shapes on paper so that they are most memorable. Using symmetry is a good way of achieving this.

Write the name of the group in the middle of the shape chosen to represent it. Note the items in each group at each corner.

Use a mnemonic to fix them

The next thing to do is make an acronym out of the items in each group. Write it around the shape, one letter at each corner. If you can make a word that means something relevant to the group concerned, this will help a great deal in storing, retaining and recalling material.

Join up the shapes

Join up the shapes in a way that makes sense. Here is an example. Suppose you are studying economics. Imagine you are setting out to memorise knowledge under the heading of aspects of production. You have worked out that the knowledge you need to absorb can be divided into six main groups:

- types of production
- division of labour
- types of growth of firms
- reason for growth
- economies of scale
- diseconomies of scale.

Suppose, also that each of these groups can, themselves, be divided into sub-groups as follows:

Types of production
- primary production
- secondary production
- tertiary production.

Sub-groups of division of labour category
- levels of specialisation
- advantages of division of labour

- disadvantages of division of labour.

Reasons for growth of firms
- economies of scale
- market dominance
- product differentiation.

Types of growth
- horizontal integration
- vertical integration
- lateral integration.

Economies of scale
- physical or technical economies
- marketing economies
- risk economies
- financial economies
- administrative economies

Diseconomies of scale (single category group)
Using the appropriate shapes you could come up with a studygram similar to that shown in Figure 1.

Advantages and disadvantages
The advantages of this method greatly outweigh the disadvantages, especially when used for exam revision.

Advantages
It is well established that the better you structure material before trying to store it in your head the better you will be able to recall it. This method pays a great deal of attention to structuring the material.

Secondly, this method uses a standard list of shapes for category items numbering one to ten and so it reduces the thought requirement.

Thirdly, there is an emphasis on symmetry or, at least, on the formulation of a picture with some spatial meaning. This makes the whole thing much easier to remember.

Fourthly, the use of acronyms to help you remember the items in the subcategories adds to the recall potential.

Disadvantages
One of the main disadvantages is that this method is relatively slow. However, there is no other method which will be so effective for exam revision. There is no doubt that the time expenditure required to organise your material in this way, prior to memorising it, will pay great dividends in the end. It may take more time at first, but the time will be saved by the non-necessity of subsequent learning sessions on the subject.

SUMMARY

- By chunking material we increase the amount we can store and retain.

- The size of the chunks does not affect the amount we can store. It is the number of chunks which limits it.

- Large chunks are as easy to remember as small chunks.

- Acronyms provide a useful means of chunking.

- Catchphrases are another useful device.

- Exploit the absurd.

- Shapes are useful in the process of chunking.

7
Associating

WHAT IS ASSOCIATION?

The second fundamental principle of memory enhancement is known as **association**. Association is linking ideas we are seeking to remember with ideas which are already stored. We do this automatically, of course, but then it tends to be done without reference to the need to recall the facts at will.

If we consciously take charge of the association process we can choose what to link the idea to, so that we can retrieve it easily when we want to. Example: if you were introduced to a tall man called Mr Jones, you might choose to observe that Mr Jones has long bones. It rhymes and it bears a relation to his physical appearance. It will not now be difficult to recall Mr Jones' name when you need to. Try it for yourself. Take the following list of names and attributes, or physical appearances, and make associations of each:

- Bill is a pharmacist.
- Jim is a tall, thin man.
- Sally lives in a little mining village in the Rhondda Valley.
- Jean is very keen on gardening.
- Sue is a sad looking girl.
- Bert is a small, thin man.
- Alan is a heavy drinker.
- Norman is a supervisor in a factory.
- Lionel is a student sitting his final exams.
- Julie is a school teacher.

Some types of association
Association does not have to mean associating something to a physical characteristic or a rhyming word. Associations can be made to:

- places
- things

- concepts
- shapes
- people
- smells
- sounds
- colours
- tastes
- skin sensations.

A combination of both

A comination of both deliberate chunking and association gives the best results. This is because chunking serves to increase the inflow of information and association serves to fix it in the memory. Paying attention to chunking only will ensure that a large amount of information is absorbed but there is no reason to assume it will stick. Paying attention to association only will ensure that information becomes securely stored, but the volume absorbed is likely to be no greater than if no memory techniques have been used at all.

An example of the use of both principles together is making acronyms from the first letters of each fact or idea in a group, but selecting an acronym which is in some way associated with the central idea unifying that group. If the members of a committee have the names:

- Martin
- Eddie
- Melanie
- Barry
- Elizabeth
- Rachel
- Sally

they would make up the acronym MEMBERS. This would be very useful because it involved enhanced chunking in the acronym and association in the linking of the acronym to the nature of the group itself. They are, of course, not always so easy, but with a little imagination and effort some way of combining both principles can often be found. As has been pointed out earlier, associating is the natural way in which we develop knowledge in our heads. As we link the new knowledge to knowledge already there we form what Piaget called schemata (plural of schema).

While I would recommend only techniques which are based on chunking or association, within these constraints there are variations which suit particular needs. Examples are:

- numbers – association with rhyme or shape
- words of a foreign language – association with comparative English words
- lists where order retention is necessary – make stories or poems.

PEGGING TO IMAGES

There are a number of established systems for pegging numbers to images.

Learning the code

Wennsshein's system was based on the rule that all the digits from 0 to 9 would be associated with a sound. The list is as follows:

0	S, Z, or soft C
1	T, D or TH
2	N
3	M
4	R
5	L
6	CH, J, SH, DG
7	K
8	F or V
9	P or B.

Using this principle plus the creative employment of the vowels, A, E, I, O and U and the unused consonants H, W and Y, words can be made from all the combinations of digits. Here is such a list.

0	sea	5	lady
1	tea	6	jay
2	near	7	key
3	ma	8	far
4	ray	9	pa

If you can think of more than one image, then it's the one that comes alphabetically first which should be chosen. The other you will probably need later in the series. If you don't work alphabetically you'll get confused. On the pages that follow, such a list has been compiled for you with some suggested images.

0 Sea	41 Rat
1 Tea	42 Rain
2 Ma	43 Ram
3 Mag	44 Roar
4 Rad	45 Rail
5 Lady	*for towels*
6 Jag	46 Rage
7 Cape	47 Rack
8 Far	48 RAFA (club)
9 Bag	49 Rap
10 Daz	50 Lace
11 Dad	51 Lad
12 Dan	52 Lane
13 Dam	53 Lamb
14 Dart	54 Lair
15 Dale	55 Lilo
16 Dash	56 Lash
17 Deck	57 Lake
18 Daf	58 Laugh
19 Dab	59 Lab
20 NASA	60 Chase
21 Nat	61 Chat
22 Nan	62 Chan
23 Name	*Charlie*
24 Nero	63 Chime
25 Nail	64 Char
26 Nash	65 Gel
imagine a dog (g)nashing its	66 Cheese
teeth	67 Cheque
27 Nag	68 Chaff
28 Navel	69 Chap
29 Nib	70 Case
imagine an inky nib	71 Cat
30 Maize	72 Can
31 Mat	73 Camel
32 Man	74 Car
33 Mame	75 Call
imagine someone singing a	76 Cage
famous song 'Mame'	77 Cake
34 Mare	78 Cafe
35 Mail	79 Cab
36 Mash	80 Face
37 Mac	81 Fade
38 Mafia	82 Fan
39 Map	83 Fame
40 Race	84 Fair

85 Fall
86 Fish
87 Fag
88 Five
imagine a dice landing on a five
89 Fab 1
Lady Penelope's Car
90 Base
91 Bat
92 Bam
93 Beam
94 Bar
95 Ball
96 Batch
97 Back
98 Beef
99 Babe
100 Daisies
101 Taste
102 Tarzan
103 Tease 'em
104 Tizer
105 Tassel
106 Discharge
107 Desk
108 Doze off
109 Does up
coat buttons
110 Daddies
sauce
111 Dad-dad
baby talk
112 Date on
stamp date on
113 Date him
his clothes date him
114 Tartare
sauce
115 Tidal
river
116 Dotage
parent looks at child
117 Too thick
people choosing not to go out in fog
118 Tooth of

holding up a tooth of an animal
119 Tot up
cashier totting up money
120 Tans
two bathers' suntans
121 Tent
122 Tanning
on a sun bed
123 Tan arm
a tanned arm, perhaps leaning out of a car window
124 Tenor
singer
125 Tunnel
126 Tin edge
rough edge of a tin
127 Think
a person sitting with forehead on clenched fist – thinking
128 Turn off
switching off the radio
129 Tenby
seaside
130 Thames
river
131 Tempt
holding out a cream cake to a dieter
132 Too many
doorman turning people away from a disco
133 Dim 'em
warning from oncoming driver
134 Tamer
lion tamer
135 Tamil
guerilla soldier in Sri Lanka
136 Too much
shopkeeper giving a customer some money back
137 To make
instruction book
138 Time off
person relaxing at home
139 Tamp
pipe smoker tamping down

tobacco

140 Tears

141 Tart

142 Tern
bird

143 Term
school term

144 Ta ra
northern goodbye

145 Toe rail
at foot of a bar

146 Tar edge
workman repairing the road

147 Tie rack
in a shop

148 The ref
in boxing

149 Tar rub
rubbing damaged skin with tar ointment

150 Tills
bank of tills in supermarkets

151 Talons
bird's long claws, or person's long fingernails

152 To let signs

153 Tail 'em
a cop following a robber's car

154 Tailor

155 Dull ale
cloudy pint of beer

156 Tail edge

157 To lock
arrow on lock

158 Tea leaf

159 Tulip

160 Tissues

161 T-shirt

162 Two chins
double-chinned person

163 Touching
people sitting close together on a bus

164 Two ales
choice of two different ales at a pub

165 The chair
electric chair (or use the word Teacher)

166 To church
signpost pointing to a church

167 Two cheques

168 To shave
person going to the bathroom to shave

169 The Ship
name on a pub

170 Tie case
cloth, or cardboard, case for ties

171 Two cats

172 Token
book token

173 Two combs

174 Tucker
tucker bag

175 Tackle
fishing tackle

176 Two bags of cash

177 Teacake

178 Take off
aeroplane taking off

179 Take up
slowly taking up the slack of a tow rope

180 Toffs
pretentiously snobbish people

181 Two feet

182 Tougher
soldiers square bashing

183 Two farms

184 Two fairs

185 Tefal
black saucepan

186 Two fish

187 Two forks

188 Two fives
two fists – bunches of fives

189 Two Fabs
two of Lady Penelope's Rolls Royces

190 Taps

basin or bath taps
191 Tepid
testing water temperature with elbow
192 Tip him
lorry tipping
193 Tap 'em
railway rail tapper, tapping wheels
194 Taper
cannon lighter
195 Tipple
person drinking whisky
196 Two bushes
person cutting a hedges
197 Two books
198 Two bevvies
two pints of beer
199 Two pipes
200 Nurses
201 No shirt
person with no shirt on
202 Nissan
car
203 No seam
imagine seamless stockings
204 No shore
sea going right up to cliffs
205 Nasal
speaking with a cold, or spraying a nasal spray
206 No sash
man in a dress suit holding his trousers up because he has no sash
207 No sock
person with one bare foot
208 Nose off
person having his/her nose cut off
209 Knees up
a dance
210 Gnats
211 *Natal*
Christmas in Portugal (Feliz Natal), or things connected

with birth
212 Knitting
213 Natter
two people leaning on the fence talking
214 New tar
newly tarred rood
215 No tail
guinea pig
216 Notch
217 New book
wrapping a new book
218 Native
219 New tap
replacing a tap on a bath or sink
220 Nuns
221 New nib
changing a pen nib
222 Ninian
Ninian Park Rugby Ground, Cardiff
223 Numen
Numen College, Cambridge
224 Nunnery
225 No nail
imagine a nail-less finger
226 No nosh
person peering into an empty sandwich tin
227 No neck
person without a neck
228 New navy
parade of sailors with new stylish uniforms
229 Nine pins
skittles
230 Numbs
dentist injection
231 Named
ship sliding down the slipway having just been named
232 Norman
Norman soldier
233 New mum
someone being introduced to their father's new wife

234　New mower
someone unwrapping a new lawn mower

235　Normal
a typical family with 2.4 children – absurd, yes

236　No match
a large and a small boxer in the ring together

237　Unmake
unmaking a made bed

238　Nymph

239　New mop
putting a new mop head on a handle

240　Norse
Viking

241　Nereid
a centipede

242　Neuron
a nerve cell

243　No room
No Vacancies sign at a guesthouse

244　No roar
lion who cannot roar

245　Narwhal
Arctic mammal

246　Nourish
a mother feeding a child

247　New York

248　Nerve

249　No robe
barrister looking for a mislaid robe before going into court

250　Nails
tin or box of nails

251　Nailed

252　Nolan
one of the Nolan sisters

253　No lamb
sign outside a butcher's ship saying No Lamb

254　New lorry
shiny new lorry

255　Nail hole

256　Knowledge

257　New lock
someone changing the door lock

258　Nullify

259　No lip
person with no lower lip

260　New shoes

261　New shirt

262　No washing
empty laundry basket

263　No shame
drunk behaving badly

264　No chair
table laid, but no chair

265　Unshell
peeling a prawn

266　No choo choo
mother saying this to infant as they look at an empty railway line

267　No cheque
someone going to pay a bill and finding there are no cheques left

268　Unshaven

269　No ship
sailor finding his ship has sailed without him

270　Necks

271　Nicked
police taking a villain away by the arm

272　Naggin(g)
nagging spouse

273　New comb
someone buying a new comb

274　Knocker
door knocker

275　Knuckle

276　No cash
someone turning their pockets inside out

277　Knockin(g)
knocking on a door

278　New coffee
popping the seal on a new jar of instant coffee

279 Notch up
fighter pilot marking up his hits
280 No face
person with no face
281 No feet
person with no feet
282 No fun
person with a glum face
283 Infamy
sleazy press reports relating to a politician
284 No fur
mangy dog
285 Novel
286 No fish
person with empty fishing net
287 Invoke
calling up a spirit, or citing a law or regulation
288 Unfavourable
289 Enfeeble
to weaken, by mollycoddling, perhaps
290 Neeps
Scots for turnips
291 New pet
a family playing with a new puppy
292 Nippon
ant killer – trade name
293 No beam
switching on a torch to find it doesn't work
294 Nipper
baby
295 Nepal
image of Mount Everest and monks
296 New page
sometime writing and starting a new page
297 No peak
mountain with a flat top
298 Unpaved
section of path with no paving slabs

299 Unpipe
a tap with no water and person looking underneath to find no pipe
300 Muses
301 Miss hit
hitting the ball badly in a ball game
302 Mason
stonemason at work
303 Museum
304 Miser
305 Missile
306 Massage
307 Music
308 Missive
official and serious letter
309 Mishap
someone dropping their dinner
310 Mats
set of table mats
311 Mutate
physiologist altering animal genes. Alternatively, use the word Matted (hair)
312 Mutton
313 Madam
314 Meter
parking meter
315 Metal
lump of iron
316 My dish
dish with your name on it
317 Mattock
digging implement similar to a pickaxe
318 Motif
a badge on the front of a car
319 Mud pie
320 Many
people in a crowd
321 Mint
322 Morning
sun rising
323 Minim
musical symbol

324 Minor
Morris Minor

325 Manilla
writing paper of a brownish shade

326 Menage
domestic establishment – husband, wife and children

327 Munich

328 My navy
your own navy, your own personal yacht, the crew wearing uniforms with your initials

329 Monopoly

330 Mimes
several people doing mimes

331 Marmet

332 Mormon
going round houses with Bible

333 My mum

334 Murmur

335 Mammal

336 My match
winning a tennis match

337 Mimic
someone mimicking another behind their back

338 Mummify

339 Mump
a neck swollen on one side

340 Mars

341 Mart
cattle market

342 Marine

343 Marry me
someone down on one knee proposing marriage

344 Mirror

345 Marl
piece of stone

346 Marriage
pair of wedding rings

347 Mark
dirty mark on clean garment

348 More of
somebody tucking into a second helping

349 Married
car with sign on the back 'Just Married'

350 Mills
Lancashire mills with smoke pouring from chimneys

351 Mallet

352 Mallen
man with white streak in hair

353 My mole
pet mole

354 Molar
back tooth

355 Mole hill

356 Mileage
mileometer in a car

357 Milk

358 My loaf
selecting your loaf from two left on the mat next door

359 Mailbag

360 Midges
little flies which bite

361 Midget
dwarf, or MG Midget sportscar

362 Mission
a church in jungle setting

363 Mismatch
two garments matching badly

364 Major
high-ranking soldier

365 My shell
crab pointing to his shell and telling you it is his

366 Magician

367 Magic
conjurer with wand

368 Match fair
imagine a fair where different kinds of matches are sold

369 My chap
lady pointing to her partner and saying, 'this is my chap'

370 Marks
371 Marked
someone tattooed all over
372 Mohican
373 Make mac
someone selling a new raincoat
374 My car
your car
375 Michael
Barrymore
376 My cash
*taking cash out of your pocket
and looking at it*
377 Macaque
a monkey
378 My cave
*someone pointing to a cave
where he or she lived*
379 Make up
380 Movies
381 Muffet
Miss
382 Muffin
a large sweet bun
383 My firm
the office of your employer
384 My fair
you owning a fair
385 Marvel
dried milk
386 My fish
*someone pointing to their
aquarium*
387 My folk
your family group
388 My fav'
my favourite
389 Move up
*someone climbing a ladder or
going up a class at school*
390 Maps
several in a book or case
391 Moped
392 My bin
*several dustbins outside houses
– one with your initials*

393 Embalm
394 Empire
395 Maple
syrup
396 Ambush
397 Impact
398 Mop offer
special offer on mops in a shop
399 Imbibe
400 Cases
401 Casts
plaster
402 Raisin
403 Resume
*summing up main points in a
speech or lecture*
404 Razor
405 Razzle
lively outing
406 Rose itch
person scratching roses
407 Rusk
408 Raise off
lifting a weight off the floor
409 Rosehip
410 Rites
last
411 Rotate
412 Rotten
apples, for example
413 Redeem
become absolved of guilt
414 Writer
person with a quill
415 Rota
416 Rattle
417 Reading
418 Write off
crashed car
419 Write up
report of research, for example
420 Runs
cricket
421 Rent
in jar for the rent collector
422 Rain in

rain water coming through
ceiling
423 Uranium
424 Runner
     marathon
425 Runnel
     gutter
426 Range
     cooking range
427 Rink
     ice
428 Rain off
     cricket or tennis match stopped
     due to rain
429 Run up
     pre election campaign
430 Rooms
431 Remade
     remade bed
432 Roman
     soldier
433 Raymond
     Burr
434 Rumour
     someone whispering behind
     someone else's back
435 Rammle
     rowdy drinking session
436 Rummage
     people rummaging through
     clothes on a table at a jumble
     sale
437 Remake
     tailor remaking a suit which
     doesn't fit
438 Remove
     trouble-maker being removed
     from a club
439 Ramp
440 Roars
     several lions roaring
441 Reared
442 Rare one
     large diamond
443 War room
     room where war strategies are

planned
444 We're raw recruits
     soldiers protesting their lack of
     experience to carry out a
     dangerous attack
445 Rural
     country image
446 Rare rash
447 Hairy rock
     you've found a hairy rock
448 Rarefy
     beat metal to make it less solid
     and dense
449 Rarebit
     Welsh rarebit
450 Rails
     for railway engines
451 Roulette
452 Hair loan
     lending some hair to someone
     who is bald
453 Realm
454 Roller
455 Rail wheel
     train wheel
456 Relish
457 Relic
     unearthing ancient piece of
     pottery
458 Relief
     famine relief food parcels being
     dropped by parachute
459 Roll up
     hand rolled cigarette
460 Rushes
461 Hairy shed
462 Russian
     Russian in Cossack hat
463 Rush home
464 Riser
     imagine an early riser
     awakening, getting out of bed
     and rubbing their eyes while it
     is still dark
465 Rush hill
     hillside covered with rushes

466 Re-judge
judge something again
467 Raw cheek
someone's cheeks red with cold
468 Rush off
somebody rushing off to catch train
469 Reach up
470 Racks
for wine
471 Racket
472 Work on
deciding to work on after time
473 Requiem
474 War cry
475 Oracle
476 Rickshaw
477 Raw cake
eating cake that has not been cooked
478 Weir cave
cave under weir
479 Rake up
someone raking up mown grass or hoed weeds
480 Roofs
481 Raft
482 Rave
483 Revamp
renovate or liven up
484 River
485 Ravel
composer
486 Ravage
487 Revoke
take away a right
488 Revive
489 Rave up
490 Rips
in jeans
491 Roped
roped off scene of crime, or dangerous area
492 Ripon
horse races
493 Rip 'em

someone ripping their denim jeans
494 Reaper
grim reaper with scythe
495 Ripple
496 Rubbish
497 Rebuke
someone giving a reprimand
498 Rip off
complaining about the cost of a meal
499 Rip up
person ripping up paper
500 Laces
501 Last
502 Loosen
someone loosening their belt, perhaps after a meal
503 Lyceum
school in ancient Athens
504 Laser
505 Lazily
506 Low sash
person with a sash around hips instead of waist
507 Lusaka
capital of Zambia
508 Lucifer
509 List
510 Lots
draw lots
511 Looted
shop with broken window and goods scattered by escaping thieves
512 Luton
small furniture van
513 Lead arm
someone with a lead arm
514 Lighter
515 Little
516 Old age
517 Low dyke
deep ditch
517 Old Turk
518 Low Taff

low water in the river Taff at
Cardiff
519 Light up
520 Lanes
   in the road
521 Linnet
   bird
522 Linen
523 Loan M
   large letter M on its own,
   perhaps like the M in the
   McDonald's fast food sign
524 Loner
   person drinking alone at a bar
525 Lineal
   in direct line of ancestry
526 Launch
527 Link
   chain link
528 Lane five
   fifth lane on a running track
529 Line up
   a line of people on parade
530 Limes
   tree full of them
531 Limit
   speed limit sign
532 Lemon
533 Lame mare
534 Lima
535 Lime ale
   drink made with lime
536 Eel match
   someone matching pairs of eels
   for size
537 Oily mack
538 Lymph
   colourless body fluid
539 Lamp
540 Lorries
541 Lard
542 Learn
   a pupil in school
543 Leiria
   city in Northern Portugal
544 Love forever

wedding
545 Laurel
546 Oil rush
   rush of prospectors to area
   rumoured to have oil
547 Laughs
   several people laughing
548 Larva
549 Oily road
550 Lilies
551 Oil light
   on dashboard of car
552 Ley line
553 Lie low aim
   soldier lying on stomach aiming
   a rifle
554 Oil lorry
   oil tanker
555 Low lolly
   ice lolly almost sucked to
   nothing
556 Low latch
   on door so low you have to sit
   down to it
557 Lilac
558 Low life
559 Lullaby
560 Lychees
   Chinese fruit
561 Low jet
562 Legion
563 Oily shammy
   wiping windscreen with a
   shammy only to leave oily
   smears
564 Lodger
565 Oil shale
566 All Jewish
567 Logic
568 Oily shave
   shaving with motor oil instead
   of shaving foam
569 Oil ship
   tanker
570 Lakes
571 Locket

572 Lycca
primitive plant life
573 Locum
temporary doctor
574 Loco
575 Local
pub
576 Luggage
577 Low kick
football kick low into the goal
578 Low cave
cave below sea level
579 Lock-up
garage or shop
580 Leaves
581 Leave it
someone who does not like their food
582 Lovin'
583 Alluvium
deposit of soil left after flood
584 Lever
585 Lovell
Sir Bernard
586 Oily fish
herring, mackerel, trout
587 Oily fork
fork used for eating oily fish
588 Leaf off
leaf off a rubber plant lying beside it
589 Lifebuoy
590 Lips
591 Lipid
592 Lap in(g)
water
593 Low beam
dipped headlights
594 Leaper
person leaping
595 Lapel
596 Lay patch
patching hole in tarred drive
597 Lie back
reclining in car seat
598 Leap off
leaping off cliff
599 Lap up
cat drinking saucer of milk
600 Cheeses
imagine several
601 Chew soap
someone chewing soap
602 Jason
leader of Argonauts in Greek legend
603 Chase me
child or dog playing tag
604 Chaser
whisky with a pint of beer
605 Chisel
606 Jazz show
607 Chiswick
flyover
608 Joseph
with coat of many colours
609 Cheese pies
610 Shades
sunglasses
611 Chips
IOUs on a spike
612 Cheating
card sharps
613 Showtime
actors getting ready for show
614 Shooter
gun
615 Shuttle
Euro-star or space shuttle
616 Chat show
617 Shed key
618 Shut off
turning the water off
619 Chat up
chatting up member of the opposite sex
620 Shins
shin pads – cricket
621 Shanty
sea song
622 Shannon
Ireland's principal river

623 Show name
*people having name badges
checked as they enter a
conference hall*

624 Shiner
black eye

625 Chanel
No 5 – perfume

626 Change
coins

627 Chunk

628 Geneva

629 Chin up
*person holding his head up to
give him courage*

630 Seamus
Irishman

631 Ashamed
*person bowing their head in
shame*

632 Shaman
Asian medicine man

633 Show mummy
*telling child to show its mother
a drawing*

634 Show mare
prize mare at a show

635 Show miles
speedometer

636 Shoe match
*shoe sale with attendants trying
to match odd shoes*

637 Jamaica

638 Germ fare

639 Jump

640 Shares

641 Shirt

642 Shorn
shorn sheep

643 Chair arm

644 Shearer

645 Share ale
*two people drinking from a pint
of ale with two straws*

646 Charge

647 Cherokee

648 Sheriff

649 Chirp
bird chirping

650 Shells

651 Shield

652 Shellin(g)
in war

653 Shalom
*Jewish ritual of salutation on
meeting or parting*

654 Jewellers

655 Shell oil
sign on service station

656 Geology

657 Shellac
paint

658 Shelf

659 Chilli pie
hot spicy pie

660 Judges

661 Judge tea
tea taster

662 Jejune
immature, spiritless

663 Ash jam
*jam made of ash and everyone
retching after eating it*

664 Cheshire

665 Church aisle

666 Chew judge
chewing up a judge

667 Church key
massive key

668 Judge fee
judge being paid fee

669 Shoe shop

670 Checks

671 Check it

672 Chicken

673 Check 'im
frisk for gun

674 Choker

675 Chuckle

676 Share cash
*buskers sharing out coins
collected in group session*

677 Chuck key
key securing electric drill bit

678 Chekhov
the poet

679 Check up
medical check up

680 Chaffs
birds

681 Chaffed
sore behind the knees from cold winds

682 Shaven

683 Shave me
sitting in barber's chair and asking the barber to shave you

684 Shaver
electric

685 Shovel

686 Show fish
fishmonger showing a fish to a customer

687 Shove key
shoving key across a table to someone else

688 Shave off
someone shaving off long beard

689 Shove up
imagine being asked to move along a bench

690 Chips

691 Chipped
plate

692 Chopin
pianist/composer

693 Show poem

694 Chopper

695 Chapel

696 Sheepish

697 Shop key
someone taking out key to open shop

698 Chop off
tree branch

699 Chop up
firewood

700 Cases

701 Cast
of face

702 Casino

703 Chasm

704 Kaiser
German Emperor

705 Castle

706 Cow search
villagers searching for lost cow

707 Cossack

708 Key safe
leather wallet designed for keys

709 Cusp
point at which two curves meet

710 Cats

711 Kitted
soldier kitted up

712 Kitten

713 Cat home

714 Carter
driver of cart

715 Cattle

716 Cottage

717 Coat hook

718 Coat off
person taking their coat off

719 Caught up
opponent running to catch up

720 Cans
of beans

721 Canape

722 Cannon

723 Connery

724 Corner

725 Canal

726 Corniche
Rolls Royce

727 Kinnock
Rt Hon Neil

728 Convoy

729 Canopy

730 Cones
several cones

731 Comet

732 Common
common person or common piece of ground

733 Comb me

dog asking owner to comb it

734 Camera

735 Colonel

736 Game show

737 Comic

738 Connive

two people plotting

739 Camp

740 Cars

741 Cart

742 Corn

ear of corn

743 Crum(b)

744 Curare

on poison dart

745 Coral

746 Crash

747 Crack

748 Carafe

749 Crop

of corn

750 Curl

751 Clot

752 Clan

represented by tartan

753 Calm

calm sea

754 Clear

empty road

755 Galileo

756 Collage

757 Clock

758 Cliff

759 Clip

paper clip

760 Catches

catches in cricket

761 Catch it

catch it toy

762 Kitchen

763 Cashmere

luxury wool

764 Catcher

rat catcher

765 Cudgel

766 Key judge

most influential of panel of judges

767 Cat choc

chocolate cat

768 Kiss Eve

769 Cap

770 Corks

771 Cooked

772 Cocoon

773 Cook

ham on spit

774 Cooker

775 Cackle

of hens

776 Corkage

bringing your own wine to a pub and paying corkage

777 Kayak cover

778 Cow cave

cave where cows sleep

779 Kick up

football

780 Coffers

money chests

781 Caveat

legal warning

782 Coffin

783 Caveman

784 Caver

785 Cavell

Nurse Cavell

786 Cafe show

show pictures in cafe

787 Cave key

map of cave system

788 Cry Viva

people at celebration crying Viva – meaning long life

789 Carve up

road abuse

790 Capes

791 Carpet

792 Coupon

793 Cow poem

poem about cows

794 Cooper

man making barrels
795 Cables
796 Cabbies
797 Kopeck
Russian coin
798 Cape off
someone taking cape off
799 Cobweb
800 Faces
801 Face up
card turned face up
802 Fission
nuclear power station
803 Fish meal
804 Fissure
fold in brain cortex
805 Facial
*woman being given facial
beauty creams*
806 Visage
stern face
807 Whiffy sock
smelly sock
808 Wave save
*estuary barrier for harnessing
wave energy to make electricity*
809 Fused
*blackened electric bulb
indicating that it is fused*
810 Fats
*meat fat, together with
potatoes on plate*
811 Faded
faded jeans
812 Fatten
cow or pig
813 Fathom
814 Future
spaceships
815 Fatal
dead person
816 Footage
newsprint
817 Fatigue
tired person
818 Photo of...

*photo with caption box for the
owner to fill in*
819 Feet up
person with feet up on chair
820 Fans
821 Faint
822 Finnan
smoked haddock
823 Venom
824 Veneer
*high quality outer surface,
often stuck onto wood furniture*
825 Funnel
826 Finish
827 Pfennig
small German coin
828 Phone wave
*radio waves emitting from
mobile phone*
829 Phone up
someone phoning
830 Forms
831 Vomit
832 Foreman
833 For me
*asking postman as he hands
you parcel*
834 Farmer
835 Female
836 Fame shy
*someone who avoids the
limelight*
837 Farm key
838 Half move
*someone going to make a chess
move and changing their mind*
839 Fumed
person who got cross
840 Firs
fir trees
841 Fought
842 Fern
843 Firm
844 Furore
anger
845 Frail

846 Fresh

847 Fork

848 Hoover off
vacuum some crumbs off chair

849 Ford
car

850 Fells
mountainsides

851 Felt
type of cloth

852 Fallen
apples on floor

853 Flame

854 Filler
for repairing car body

855 Fill well
filling a well with bucket

856 Hoof show
a show of horses' hooves

857 Flack
fallout from gunfire

858 Fall off
something falling off lorry

859 Fill up
car at petrol station

860 Fudges
several fudge sweets

861 Fidget
someone fidgeting

862 Fashion

863 Heysham
Lancashire village with nuclear power station

864 Forger
making counterfeit money

865 Fudge Hill
hill made of fudge, in which your feet sink as you climb

866 Fish shop

867 Hive shack
shack looking like a beehive

868 Fetch food

869 Fish pie

870 Fakes
fake ten pound notes

871 Fate

872 Wave Cane
someone waving cane

873 Vacuum

874 Fakir
Muslim or Hindu religious person

875 Fickle
changeable person

876 Have cash
realising you have enough cash to pay a bill

877 For cake
flour

878 Have coffee

879 Fork pea
spearing a pea with your fork

880 Fyfe's
banana boat

881 Furry foot

882 Five new
five new members of group

883 Heave home
oarsmen being coaxed to heave on to get home

884 Fiver
five pound note

885 Half full
half full beer glass

886 Half fish

887 Half awake
somebody half awake so goes back to sleep

888 Vivify
to animate

889 Half pie

890 Few peas

891 Half pot
half a saucepan

892 Few pins

893 Fed 'em
chicken farmer returning home

894 Feeder
feeder canal

895 Fable

896 Foppish

897 Hay pack

pack of hay for horse

898 Food off
the food is off

899 Fed up
sitting looking glum

900 Paces
walking three paces

901 Passes
car passes another

902 Poison

903 Possum

904 Pizza

905 Parcel

906 Passage

907 Basic

908 Pass off
fake goods

909 Pass up
let an opportunity go

910 Pets

911 Petite
small, slim woman

912 Pattern
knitting pattern

913 Bottom

914 Peter
anyone who know of this name

915 Petal

916 Potage
plants in greenhouse

917 Optic

918 Put off
decline to buy goods

919 Potted
potted meat

920 Pans

921 Paint

922 Pining
pining dog

923 Pin 'em
tailor pinning trousers for alterations

924 Banner

925 Panel
of car

926 Panache

person with style

927 Panic
frightened person

928 Wipe knife

929 Pin up
photo

930 Pimms
the drink

931 Wipe mat

932 Bowman

933 Be mum
saying which means pour the tea

934 Be merry

935 Pummel
person beating clothes with stick

936 Beam show
show of dancing beams

937 Beam hook
hook on beam of house

938 Beam off
car switching headlights off

939 Beam up
character in film being beamed up to spaceship

940 Bulbs
row of bulbs

941 Fort

942 Bathin(g)
someone bathing

943 Bathe arm
someone bathing cut arm

944 Bath half
small house, half bathroom and half living area

945 Bee vale
valley with loads of beehives in it

946 Purge

947 Pork

948 Be rough
wrestler being rough in wrestling ring

949 Prop
clothes prop

950 Pals
951 Pelt
someone throwing stones
952 Plan
953 Palm
954 Pallor
a pale skin
955 Pull ale
bar person pulling pint
956 Pillage
piracy
957 Pillock
stupid person
958 Pull off
pulling off sock
959 Pull up
doing pull ups
960 Pages
961 Paged
a person contacted by pager
962 Pigeon
963 Push me
asking someone to push you on a swing
964 Pitcher
water vessel
965 Bushel
966 Bushes
several bushes
967 Be shook
someone shaking you
968 Push off
telling someone to push off
969 Push by
pushing by people in crowd
970 Picks
pickaxes
971 Pickets
picket line
972 Peckin(g)
chickens pecking
973 Pigmy
974 Poker
975 Piccolo
976 Packets
977 Peacock
978 Pick off
somebody picking paint off their skin
979 Perk up
person suddenly looking happier
980 Paths
several paths leading in different directions
981 Pippup
seesaw
982 Pavin(g)
983 Be famous
984 Be fair
a judge
985 Be full
feeling full after large meal
986 Bi-vision
pair of bifocal spectacles
987 Pave kerb
workman paving kerb at side of road
988 Be favoured
person being treated favourably at work and arousing jealousy
989 Beef up
slow song being played fast
990 Pipes
991 Pipette
laboratory instrument for sucking up small amounts of liquid
992 Pop in
neighbour popping in for a chat
993 Pop 'em
person squeezing spots
994 Paper
995 Papal
the Pope's robes
996 Pipage
lots of pipes around the room
997 Pop corns
998 Pipe off
looking under a sink to see why there is no water and finding pipe removed
999 Pipe up
person speaks up in a group

Utilising the list

When you have learned the list thoroughly, you will be in a position to easily remember 15 digit numbers after hearing them only once. This is because people can easily remember seven plus or minus two items. If we have chunked each set of three digits into one unit (*ie* an image) we will be able to recall between 15 (5 x 3) and 27 (9 x 3) numbers. A reader of average intelligence can expect to reach at least the low end of the range, *ie* 5 items and, therefore, 5 x 3 digits, which, of course, is 15.

Using this vocabulary of images, you will be able to memorise and recall very long numbers. What you do is you form an immediate image after every three digits have been heard or read. You link the images together into a story. The links should be simple, for example, the images may:

- be stuck together
- one placed on top of another
- bump into one another
- hold hands.

Advantages

One of the main advantages of this method is that once you have learned the master vocabulary you can formulate your images quite quickly. Secondly, you can randomly access particular portions of the number, rather than having to chug through from start to finish.

USING THE METHOD OF LOCI

The oldest known method of association is known as the **method of loci**.

The ancient Greek sophists (travelling teachers) would memorise important parts of their lectures by mentally associating them with rooms in a house or building they knew. They would spend time walking around the insides of buildings so that they had a store of different ones – one for each lecture. They would associate the important points in their lectures with parts of one of these buildings. As they gave their lectures, they would mentally walk through the relevant buildings recalling each theme as they walked from room to room.

The Roman room system

Later, the Romans developed a slightly different system. It involved just one room – a fantasy one. It has since been known as the **Roman room system**.

They would dream up a room and keep it as their memory aid. This room would contain items of furniture and other things, but would not be too cluttered. When they wished to remember anything, they would mentally hang the details on the items in the room.

This can be useful for remembering ideas in sequence, because you can imagine hanging things in a particular order. Here is an example. Suppose you wanted to remember to go to the bank, buy some rail tickets, take books back to the library, phone your friend and then keep an optician's appointment. Suppose, too, in the private Roman room in your mind you have a coat stand, a table, four dining chairs, a desk and a chair. You might mentally hang a banknote on one of the coat hooks on the stand. After this you might place the rail tickets on one of the chairs. Next, you might open the library books on the table and, perhaps, mentally stamp them with a library stamp. You might, then, sit on the office chair and talk to your friend on the phone. Imagine, then, that you see the appointment book on the desk. You can't quite make out what it says and you fumble about in the drawer for your spectacles.

THE NUMBER SHAPE SYSTEM

The **number shape system** is a method of remembering numbers by associating them with a shape.

A figure one is like a pen and a figure two is like a swan. A figure three is like a pair of spectacles, which have fallen onto a railway line and been cut in half. A figure four is like a yacht, or at least that part above the hull. Here is a full list of suggested images, from zero to nine.

0	A lake	6	A yo-yo
1	A pen	7	A boomerang
2	A swan	8	A lady with an hour glass
3	Spectacles cut in half		figure
4	A yacht	9	A sunflower
5	An anvil		

When you wish to memorise a long number, just make a story out of these images. Here is an example. The number 3543165789 can be memorised by associating and linking the digits as follows: A half pair of spectacles were lying on a blacksmith's anvil. He must have been trying to repair them. They had been run over by a yacht, he said. 'Quite straight is the keel of a yacht. Here is the other half.' He took out a pen, knocked it through the centre of a yo-yo and then he jammed it into a hole in the top of the anvil – to fix the halves of the specs around, perhaps. Then he took a tool which looked like a boomerang and heated it until it was red hot. Then he used it to weld the two pieces of the specs together. He then gave the glasses back to a lady who had brought them to be mended and she gave him a sunflower in exchange.

THE NUMBER RHYME SYSTEM

The **number rhyme system** works on a similar principle, except that we make associations on the basis of rhyme. One rhymes with bun, for example. Two rhymes with shoe and three rhymes with tree. Here is a full list of rhyming images from zero to ten.

0	Fort	5	Hive
1	Bun	6	Sticks
2	Shoe	7	Devon
3	Tree	8	Gate
4	Door	9	Pine
		10	Hen

If you have a number to remember, you just associate the digits with these images and build a story.

Consider, for example, the number 361512839. This could be memorised by making up the following story, using the images given.

A person tries to build a tree with sticks. He uses a bun as the base and puts a beehive against the stack to hold it up. Then he puts another bun on the top, securing it by bashing it onto the upright sticks with a shoe. Then he goes out through the gate, turns around and the tree is whole again, but it has changed from an oak to a pine.

Now try it for yourself. Memorise the following digits in order. Draw the images you use, then go away and do something different. Come back in ten minutes and test yourself to see how well you did. There are ten digits so each represents 10 per cent of a 100 per cent recall score.

3, 6, 5, 4, 3, 1, 8, 2, 9, 5

THE ALPHABET SYSTEM

The **alphabet system** is for remembering letters of the alphabet. It can help with spellings. It works by linking permanently in your mind short words starting with each letter of the alphabet. The words should obviously start with the letter itself. This should be followed by the earliest letter of the alphabet available to make a monosyllabic word. Use a dictionary for this; it will make the task even easier. Here is an example list.

A Ace	H Hag	O Oak	V Vat
B Bee	I Ice	P Pad	W Wag
C Cab	J Jab	Q Q(u)ad	X Xmas
D Dab	K Keg	R Rag	Y Yard
E Eat	L Lab	S Sac	Z Zap
F Fag	M Mad	T Tab	
G Gag	N Nag	U Up	

Remember to exercise both sides of the brain, the sequential processing left hemisphere and the spatial processing right hemisphere, as you build your stories. Use all the sense impressions, and exploit qualities such as humour, exaggeration, and so on.

Furthermore, the first connections, associations, or rhymes that spring to mind are often the best. Stories with personal meanings are very useful. Stories or statements relating directly to the essence of the material being memorised are particularly so.

Remember, also, that your linkings between the images should be simple. (See page 99.)

Rehearsing the story

It is not sufficient to simply build a story. You have to rehearse it. This amounts to some degree of **overlearning**. There is evidence that overlearning strengthens the memory trace and aids recall. Indeed, this is why actors and actresses go over their lines time and time again.

Making poems instead of stories

The technique for making poems is basically the same as for making stories, except that you include rhythm and, in these kinds of poems, rhyme. Poems are easier to remember than stories. Indeed, they were used as memory aids before most people became literate enough to write things down. In oral cultures, knowledge was carried over from generation to generation by means of poems and maxims. The latter did not always have rhyme, but it tended to have rhythm.

Making things rhyme
Sometimes you have to force rhyme. There is nothing wrong with this, poets do it all the time. Forcing rhyme means choosing words that almost rhyme, but not quite.

BUILDING IMAGES INTO PICTURES

An alternative to building images into stories is to build them into pictures. You can create a whole scene or landscape and carry that in your head into the exam room. Instead of running through a story containing your images, scan from top left to bottom right of the picture, recalling each image and the idea it represents as you go.

Alternatively, you can build a dynamic picture. What is meant here is a picture of a scene where things are going on. It may be a battle scene and several characters and elements of the picture are playing different roles. Or it could be a street scene, where different people are rushing about performing their different roles: the postman delivering letters, the policeman directing traffic, the taxi driver picking up a fare, workmen working in a trench in the road and a doorman attending the doors of a hotel.

Formulating the images
Remember the three main principles for image making:

- make them striking
- make them concrete
- make them dynamic.

Making them striking
You make images striking by exaggerating their qualities, as a cartoonist does. Paint them in brilliant cartoon-like colours:

- if they are large make them larger
- if they are small make them smaller
- if they are fat make them fatter
- if they are thin make them thinner
- if they are sharp make them sharper
- if they are angry make them angrier
- if they are jolly make them jollier.

Making them concrete
Avoid vague images in your picture-making. Use only down-to-earth, everyday objects.

Making them dynamic
Your pictures should indicate movement. A bustling scene is better than a quiet and still landscape.

The first to spring to mind are often the best
The first pictures which spring to mind are often the best. This will, to some degree, be due to the fact that if you reject the first picture to come to mind and choose another, there will be some retroactive interference from the first picture you thought of. Retroactive interference is distortion of stored material as a result of materials stored previously. If you reject one idea after another before deciding on a picture, your stored picture will be subject to several sources of distortion.

Exploiting the absurd
Remember that we tend to recall humorous things best. Don't forget, therefore, to exploit the absurd in your picture.

Advantages and disadvantages
As with all memory techniques, there are advantages and disadvantages.

Advantages
One of the main advantages of a visual representation over a verbal one is that you can scan the whole picture more or less at once. With a story, however, you have to chug through it from start to finish. Random access to material is, therefore, more readily available in visual representation.

Some people will feel more at home building a picture than building a story. It depends where their best talents lie.

Disadvantages
Some people may find it a little difficult to decide where to put each image in the picture. In contrast, the story method does not present such dilemmas. The sequence in which you link things must be the sequence in which you hear or see them. This sequential method of linking can, however, also be used in formulating a picture.

REMEMBERING TELEPHONE NUMBERS

Isn't it annoying that whenever someone wants to give you their phone number you find you haven't a pen and neither has anyone else? Then there are times when you jot it down on a scrap of paper and lose the paper. Times like that won't be a problem if you master the memory techniques contained in this book. It's still a good idea to put telephone numbers in your personal directory as soon as you can, though. The memory tricks won't guarantee that the numbers remain recallable forever.

Again, use the major image vocabulary given on pages 80–98, the number rhyme system, or the number shape system. Here is an example. Suppose you have to remember a friend's telephone number – 121250. In the major image vocabulary 121 represents a tent and 250 a Norseman (Viking). Imagine a tent with your friend wearing a Viking helmet peeping out of the flap.

Alternatively, you could imagine your friend indulging in a superstitious ritual of taking a bun out of each of his shoes and placing them in a beehive to cure a wart. Remember the **number rhyme system** – 1 is a bun, 2 is a shoe, 5 is a hive, 0 can be a wart in this case.

The **number shape system** could also be used. Imagine your friend prodding two ducks along the road with two sticks until he arrives at the blacksmith's shop. Here he drops an anvil on them and puts them in the pot to cook.

Mental organiser/diary

Use the major image vocabulary on pages 80 to 98 to give a number to the hour. For example, 9am invokes the image of a bag. Imagine this image in the context of an appointment you have to keep. Suppose you have to see your bank manager at 9am. Imagine carrying a large bag of money into the bank to see him. Feel how heavy it is. Smell the mustiness of the cloth. Hear it rustle and jingle. Feel the heat of the cloth under your hand, as you change hands. Feel the warmth of the bank as you go in and hear the counting of money and the smell of polish and fresh flowers. Suppose your next appointment is with your dentist, at 10 o'clock. Imagine collecting some cash from the bank as you walk out. You need it to buy a packet of Daz (the image for 10) at the supermarket on the way. You intend to wash the dentist's drills in it before he or she touches your mouth with them. Feel the smell of the powder as you do this. Hear it pouring out. Hear the dentist's protestations as you do so.

Suppose your third appointment is a 2 o'clock (14.00 hours) lunch appointment with a friend, Pauline. Imagine yourself thinking all the way from the dentist that you will not be able to eat your lunch because of the numbness of your gum. You find a dart (the image for 14) in your pocket and you prick your gums to see if the feeling has come back. You find it has not. You think to yourself that if you cannot eat Pauline will be able to because she is 'poor' and 'lean' (Pauline). She needs to be built up (you imagine her as poor and thin).

Lorayne's method of remembering weekdays of dates in the current year

Memory tricks can impress people at parties. Harry Lorayne set out a method for quickly calculating the day of the week for any date in the current year.

You simply have to memorise the number 411537526416. You can use the images provided in the major image vocabulary. For example, imagine rotating (swinging round) an oily mack and then launching it into the air. You become surprised to find that it rattles as it flies.

- 411 Rotate
- 537 Oily mack
- 526 Launch
- 416 Rattle

Each of the 12 digits in the number are the dates on which the first Sunday of each month fall. For example, in January the first Sunday falls on the 3rd, in February it falls on the 7th, and so on. If you want to know on what day of the week the 29th February falls you just add as many sevens as you can to the number 7 without exceeding the number 29. In other words add 3 x 7 and you get to 28. 28, therefore, is a Sunday. The 29th must be a Monday.

REMEMBERING HISTORICAL DATES

Dates of important historical events can be memorised by making a relevant word out the sounds represented by the digits (see page 79). For example, using the sounds that represent the digits in the rules underlying the major image vocabulary, the date of the First World War started – 1914 – could be remembered by the phrase, tub of tar:

- 1 is represented by T (or D)
- 9 is represented by B (or P)
- 1 is, again represented by T (or D)
- 4 is represented by R.

Two phonetically spelt words TuB and TaR can be formed (remember you can use whatever vowels you like). Imagine the Prime Minister of one country tipping a tub of tar over the shoes of the Prime Minister of the other country, thus starting the war.

Exercise
Try to think of ways of memorising the following dates:

- 1066 – The Norman Conquest
- 1189 – Start of the reign of Richard I
- 1215 – Signing of the Magna Carta
- 1399 – The start of the reign of Henry IV
- 1688 – James II deposed.
- 1702 – The start of the reign of Queen Anne
- 1776 – Adam Smith published *The Wealth of Nations*.

Remember, use all your senses in the images and make them relevant to the context. Make the connections simple and make them striking.

LEARNING LANGUAGES

Learning languages can be made easier by the use of association. Here are some examples.

In Portuguese the word *encima* means on top of. I find it easy to think of sitting in the cinema and imagining the light from the projector overhead – on top of – the audience. The word for beard is *barber*. Imagine a man going to a barber to have his beard trimmed. There are texts which suggest learning languages using systems of stories and rhymes. Avoid these. You don't get time to run through stories and rhymes when you are trying to think of a word in conversation.

MEMORISING LONG NUMBERS

If you need to remember long numbers, the major image vocabulary based on Wennsshein's system, provided on pages 80 to 98 can be

very useful. For example, let's deal with the number 360489297.
Using the image vocabulary we could build a story as follows:

A Martian jumps into the sea. A rescuer follows with a pole.
A navy patrol comes.

You could also use the number rhyme system, or the number shape
system. However, they are by no means ideal, because the story of
images will be so long that it will, itself, be hard to remember.

Using the number rhyme system
If we were to use this system, we might build a story as follows:

A tree (3) collapses into sticks (6) but they are all caught (0) in
a net hooked onto the door (4). They will be used to make a
new gate (8) on which there will be a red line (9) and nailed to
it will be a shoe (2) which will also bear a red line (9) with an
arrow pointing to Devon (7).

Just compare the complexity of this with the simplicity of using the
major image vocabulary. The beauty of the latter is that it chunks
the numbers in threes, leaving only three units to be memorised
rather than 15. It becomes, therefore, dead easy.

Exercise
Now try it for yourself with the following numbers:

356924153
295431658
397276340
898872531
295453162

When you have proved to yourself that you can recall these numbers
with the page covered, wait ten minutes and prove to yourself that
you can still remember them. Test yourself again after a day. You'll
be amazed.

CARD MEMORY

Would you like to be a really good card player? The big money
games rely a great deal on being able to guess what cards are in the

other players' hands. This involves also trying to remember what has already been put down. But how can you do all this *and* still try to judge the other players' expressions *and* play your own hand skilfully? Some people can. How do they do it?

Here's one way and it's very powerful. In a pack of playing cards you have four suits:

- Hearts
- Diamonds
- Spades
- Clubs.

In each of these there are cards numbered two to ten, plus a Jack, a Queen, a King and an Ace. The latter has a numerical value of one or eleven. All you have to do is learn this set of associations. It is not very long, so it won't be difficult. It is based on the sound associations of Wennsshein's system. As you see each card come out of the pack, connect the associated image to the image of the previous card. Do it in such a way that you are continuously building a story in your mind. This way you will at least be able to assess what is not in the other players' hands. Thus, by deduction, you can achieve a better guess of what is. Couple this with the degree of risk the other players seem prepared to take, and the nature of their expressions and you will have a definite edge.

Here is the list of images:

Hearts		*Diamonds*	
1	Hat	1	Dart
2	Hen	2	Den
3	Ham	3	Dam
4	Hair	4	Door
5	Hill	5	Dale
6	Hedge	6	Dash
7	Hake (fish)	7	Deck
8	Heave (imagine people lifting)	8	Daffy (daffodil)
9	Heap	9	Dip
10	Hose	10	Daz (washing powder)
J	Hedge	J	Disk jockey
Q	Headquarters	Q	Duck quill
K	Hack (type of horse)	K	Doctor

Spades		Clubs	
1	Seat	1	Cat
2	Sun	2	Can
3	Samba (lively Latin-American dance)	3	Comb
4	Sari	4	Car
5	Sale	5	Coil
6	Sash	6	Cage
7	Sack	7	Cake
8	Safe	8	Cave
9	Soap	9	Cap
10	Sauce	10	Case
J	Siege	J	Joke
Q	Squire	Q	Quake
K	Sack	K	Kick

Party tricks with cards

There are party tricks you can do with cards if you have developed an enhanced memory.

As someone calls out, or shows, each card in turn you imagine the image and build a story. Make sure you include all the senses in the images. For example, suppose the first card was the ace of hearts. See the colour of the hat; touch it and feel its texture. Feel the lightness on your head. Hear the sound as you rub your finger over the felt.

If the next card is the three of diamonds, feel the wind blowing at your hat, as you stand and look over the dam. Hear the water and see the glistening colours. Smell the freshness of the water.

If the next card is the six of clubs, see a budgerigar cage floating in the water. Hear the budgie chirping and try to reach it, just touching it with your fingers, as you try to hook it in. Imagine the fear the budgie is feeling.

Always exaggerate the images and make the forms dramatic. With a bit of practice, you will be able to memorise an entire pack of cards so that you can recall each one blindfolded.

SPELLING

A number of words are habitually misspelt in the English language. It will be useful to find a way of always getting them right. Rhyme lends itself well to this purpose. For example, two such words are *accommodation* and *address*. People tend to leave the double *m* and double *d* out of them. One way to master this forever is to remember the rhyme:

Accommodation and address
have a double c, d, m and s.

Another example is the *i* before *e* except after *c* rule.

The silent n

Some words have a silent *n* at the end. Because of this, they are among the most commonly misspelt words in the English language. Here are some such words:

Column
Solemn
Condemn
Autumn.

Think of this statement:

Nelson is solemn,
Because his column,
Is condemned to be demolished
In the autumn.

This will remind you of those words to which this provision applies.

Interesting letters

Anxious is another word which people commonly misspell. As you would expect, people have no difficult with the *an*, it's the rest of the letters which are the problem. Memorise this statement and you will have no more difficulty with this word.

I am anxious because I O(owe)U(you) some money
and you look X (cross).

It will be obvious where the *x* goes. The rest of the letters are in the right order. This spelling is easy to remember with this memory trick and nobody should ever have trouble with this word again.

Disappear is another problematic word. People tend to omit one of the *p*'s. Just keep in mind the warning – *don't let one of the p's disappear*.

SUMMARY

- We naturally use association to store things in long-term memory.

- We can increase the effectiveness of this process by taking conscious control of the association process.

- Combine association with chunking for maximum efficacy.

- Peg to images.

- Learn and use an image code.

- The method of loci and the Roman room system are useful where retention of order is important.

- Number rhyme and number shape methods are useful for remembering numbers and require relatively little mental preparation.

DISCUSSION POINTS

1. Do you make associations to commit things to memory?

2. What is the nature of the images you think work best? Why?

3. Which of the association strategies described in this book would seem to be the best to you and why? Do you think some are best for some things and others for others?

4. Why should exploiting the absurd be useful?

5. Consider what you think the advantages and disadvantages might be of the association methods described in this book.

6. Are you better at visio-spatial images, or sequential (story or poem-like) images? Why do you think this is so?

8
Using Memory Techniques Sensibly

Memory techniques should be regarded as an aid not a crutch. They will enable you to absorb and retain information, but will not help you understand it.

LEARNING EFFECTIVELY

Simply absorbing material teaches you little or nothing. You need to engage with the knowledge to bring about an interaction between what you already know and what you are learning.

There is no point in cluttering your head with knowledge if you don't understand what it means. This is what happens as a result of parrot-fashion learning, or cramming.

You won't be able use it effectively
You may go into the exam room with lots of facts, but when you come to try to apply them to the questions, you won't know how. To take in knowledge usefully, you have to get to grips with it and understand it.

Schemata building – mental processing
The eminent psychologist, Piaget, has provided us with an understanding of how learning takes place in the mind. Each experience we take in through our senses we compare with stored experience already in our heads. The latter we call **schemata** (the plural of schema). These stored experiences exist as patterns of neural connections.

When we encounter new material through our senses we do two things with it. Firstly, we modify the patterns which are already in our heads, to some degree, to help accommodate the new material. Secondly, we change what we are experiencing, *ie* seeing or hearing, to some degree, to complete the fit.

By deliberately attending to the association process as, indeed, we do when we exercise a trained memory, we are enhancing the natural process of schemata development.

Investigating
According to the two process model of memory, information passes from short-term memory to long-term memory when we do something with it. The level of processing theory also provides that processing is the key to long-term storage. If we investigate any knowledge we are taking in, in some way or another, we increase the degree of processing and therefore, strengthen the storage.

Comparing
One of the things we can do with incoming information is to deliberately compare it with other information we have.

Contrasting
The counter side of comparing is contrasting. By deliberately finding contrasts with any knowledge we are taking in, we strengthen the trace still further.

Evaluating evidence
If we take information in as fact, we assume there is evidence and we should want to satisfy ourselves that this is so. We should be sceptical about such evidence until we have evaluated it for ourselves. This, too, will strengthen the memory trace.

Understanding the variables and models
Often, we take in knowledge without fully understanding every bit of it. If we focus on each individual part and make sure we understand its nature, we are, again, intensifying the storage process in another way.

Models are ways of explaining or understanding knowledge. We should ask ourselves whether there are other models, or ways of understanding this which we have not yet encountered.

Distinguishing between fact, opinion and belief
Another way of engaging with any knowledge we are taking in is to consider its nature. Is it actual fact we are taking in, or is it opinion, or belief? Facts are supported by evidence. Opinions are favoured interpretations and beliefs are stored predications, that is, acceptances that *something is something*.

WHAT MEMORY TECHNIQUES CAN'T DO

There are many wild claims made for memory techniques, including that they can actually increase your IQ. Take no notice. They cannot.

They can't replace learning

Nor can memory techniques replace learning. They are not a cop out of education.

They can, however, be used to store lots of information which you may wish to manipulate from memory. They can also be used to store lots of facts which you have already ensured you understand. You can then use them without reference to a textbook in an exam, or other situation.

Analysis and synthesis

Effective learning depends on analysis and synthesis.

Analysis

Analysis involves separating material into categories or classes. There are many ways that you'll be able to do this and it requires some creativity and imagination. Memory techniques will not replace this process.

Synthesis

Synthesis is the recombination of separate categories, for example, after analysis. This recombination will always be carried out on the basis of some kind of sense. Categories will be brought together for a rational purpose, to enhance understanding of something or other. Memory techniques cannot replace this process.

Criticality

Everybody should adopt the stance of intelligent scepticism. It is not intellectually healthy to take any knowledge for granted just because somebody told you it, or you saw it written down. It's surprising how many people insist that something or other is absolutely right because they read it in a newspaper. Knowledge should be evaluated and criticised, and only after you have satisfied yourself that it is accurate should you accept it as useful. Memory techniques cannot do this for you.

WHAT MEMORY TECHNIQUES CAN DO

Memory techniques can, however, supercharge your learning in a very powerful way. They can also make you a much more effective person in every aspect of your life.

They can support memory

Memory techniques cannot improve memory. Your biological memory quality is determined by your genes, your physiology and, perhaps, diet and lifestyle. What memory techniques can do, however, is support your memory by training other cognitive abilities. These include: association, chunking and image formation. The final result can be as if you had an extremely superior memory.

They can increase your ability to remember and recall things many-fold

The effective use of memory techniques will not simply improve your ability to store, retain and recall information marginally. There is no doubt whatsoever that their use can enhance such ability many, many-fold.

Storing, retaining and retrieving
There are techniques which focus upon the storage part of memory. These are based on chunking. Techniques which focus upon retention are such things as periodic recall and correction. These techniques focus upon the serial reproduction effect: the natural pattern of memory effectiveness. We tend to remember the earliest parts of a series of knowledge and the most recent parts. We remember least well the middle parts. Techniques which focus upon increasing retention make a person recall and correct material in the middle parts of the series. Strategies which focus upon the retrieval aspect are based on association.

Getting more out of your time
Training your memory can make you a more effective person in many ways.

It can prevent you losing ideas for want of an opportunity to write them down. It can relieve you of having to make excuses for things you've forgotten to do. It can also save you time trying to find things you've misplaced.

Educationally

A trained memory can increase your learning ability and improve your exam performance. One of the ways it can do this is to enable you to take in considerable amounts of material and retain it for recall and consideration at more convenient times. It can also enhance your ability to absorb and retain information close to exam periods, for example, during revision, when it would otherwise be difficult to take in new facts. It hardly needs to be said that it can also greatly increase your exam performance.

Socially

Remembering people's names is an important social skill. So, of course, is remembering things about them. Both of these things give people the impression that they are important to you. Having a trained memory will, thus, enhance your social abilities and make you more confident and impressive in company.

Professionally

A trained memory can certainly benefit you in your chosen profession. This will be the case whether you deal with people, papers or machines. Companies are bound to value people who hold large stores of relevant information in their heads. You will be justifiably seen as more competent if you remember relevant processes well. If you can remember people's names and things about them, you will gain the respect and affection of colleagues on levels above and below yourself.

SUMMARY

- Memory techniques will not replace learning.

- Only things like discovery, evaluation, analysis and synthesis can provide understanding.

- By training other cognitive faculties these memory techniques can increase your ability to store, retain and recall things many-fold.

- Learning memory enhancement techniques can improve your life in terms of your career, your education, your social life and your personal development.

DISCUSSION POINTS

1. Do you think you can expect too much of memory techniques?

2. What do you think is striking the right balance?

3. Many people have seen the *Rain Man* film and the impressive memory feats the central character performs. Is this within everyone's grasp, or just some people?

4. What are the real benefits you can get out of using memory techniques?

5. Can these techniques assist learning, or just improve retention? If the former, how?

Further Reading

'Analysis of memory performance in terms of skill', K A Ericcson, in *Advances in Psychology of Human Intelligence*, R J Sternberg (ed.), vol 4, pp. 137–179 (Lawrence Earlbaum, 1988).

How to Study and Learn, P Marshall (How To Books, 1996, 2nd edn.).

'Piaget's Theory', J Piaget, in *Manual of Child Psychology* P H Mussen (ed.), (Wiley, 1970).

Superior Memory, J Wilding and E Valentine (Psychology Press, 1997).

The Psychology of the Child, J Piaget and B Inhelder (Routledge and Kegan Paul, 1969).

Your Memory, A Baddelly (Prion, 1982).

Index

Acronyms, 14, 33, 70, 71, 72, 73, 74, 75, 76, 78
Alphabet, 14, 59
Alphabet system, 102
Anxiety, 14, 15
Appointments, 14, 17
Association, 14, 22, 77
Attention, 14, 24
Attitude, 14, 25
Autobiographical memory, 14, 21, 41

Card memory, 109
Catchphrases, 36, 72
Choline, 27
Chunking, 22, 70
Clues, 21
Cognitive perspective, 22
Computing, 66
Cued recall, 60
Cues, 15, 61, 69

Dates, 106
Descartes, 17

Economics of cognitive organisation, 17
Educational, 14
Electronic organisers, 54
Emotions, 25, 26
Events, 17
Exam revision, 15, 27, 65, 75, 76

Folic acid, 27
Forgetting, 24
Formulae, 60
Functions of memory, 20

Glucose, 27

Hippocampus, 21
Hypnotism, 25

Image vocabulary, 108
Incidental memory, 21
Intelligence, 22
Intentional memory, 21
Interference, 22
Iodine, 27

Learning languages, 107
Left hemisphere, 21, 57, 102
Level of processing model, 22
Locke, John, 70
Long-term memory, 22, 40, 112

Managers, 14
Memories of processes, 21
Memory, 20
Memory for actions, 20
Memory for events, 20
Memory for intentions, 20
Memory for knowledge, 20
Memory techniques, 14

Memory training, 23
Memory tricks, 106
Mental blocks, 15, 25, 64
Method of loci, 99
Mnemonic, 74
Modular memory, 22
Morton, Tom, 18

Names, 14, 61
Neurones, 22
Number rhyme, 108
Number rhyme system, 101
Numbers, 107
Number shape system, 100, 108

Pegging, 79
Penfield, 21
Personal development, 17
Personnel staff, 14
Physical memory aids, 53
Pi constant, 18
Pictures, 103
Poems, 102
Primacy effect, 28, 47
Pro-active interference, 23
Psychoanalysis, 24

Quizzes, 17

Recall, 15
Reconstructing, 67
Reconstruction, 21
Rehearsal, 31
Remembering names, 14
Repression, 22, 23
Retention, 47
Retroactive interference, 23, 104
Revision notes, 33

Rhyme, 61
Right hemisphere, 102
Roman room system, 100
Routines, 32

Sales people, 14
Schemata, 78
Self distortions, 25
Serial reproduction effect, 28
Shapes, 44, 73
Shopping lists, 62
Short-term memory, 22
Social, 15
Spelling, 110
Story, 102
Stress, 27, 28, 56, 65
Studygrams, 33
Superior memory performance, 23
Suppressing, 25
Symmetry, 44

Telephone numbers, 16, 105
Tension, 15
Testing memory, 26
Tip of the tongue technique, 59
Trained memory, 23
Two process theory, 22
Tyrosine, 27

Unconscious mind, 65
Untrained memory, 23

Verbal material, 27
Vitamin B, 27

Whechsler scale, 26
Words, 59

MAKING A WEDDING SPEECH
How to prepare and present a memorable speech

John Bowden

At thousands of weddings each year, many people are called on to 'say a few words'. But what do you say? How do you find the right words which will go down really well with the assembled company? Written by an experienced and qualified public speaker, this entertaining book shows you how to put together a simple but effective speech well suited to the particular occasion. Whether you are the best man, bridegroom, father of the bride or other participant, it will guide you every step from great opening lines to apt quotations, anecdotes, tips on using humour, and even contains 50 short model speeches you can use or adapt to any occasion.

166pp. 1 85703 347 7. 3rd edition.

UNLOCKING YOUR POTENTIAL
How to master your mind, life and destiny

Peter Marshall

Even the smartest individuals will not fulfil their potential on intellect alone. If you really want to unlock your potential and become master of your own life, you will need to remove the barriers to success: your own narrow expectations, and those imposed by others. This book will show you how to do it. It will introduce you to techniques for overcoming the limiting effects of the past: conditioning, misguided or obsolete teachings and repressed conflicts. You will learn how to develop your creativity, improve your ability to solve problems, and manage your social contacts to facilitate success. An invaluable book for people from all walks of life who want to change their lives for the better and have the courage to break down the walls that hold them back. Peter Marshall is a member of the Applied Psychology Research Group of the University of London and specialises in mind and memory development. He is also author of *How to Study and Learn* and *Research Methods* in this series.

144pp. 1 85703 252 7.

THRIVING ON STRESS
How to manage pressures and transform your life

Jan Sutton

The pressures of modern life make us susceptible to stress. However not all stress is negative – if managed effectively we can positively thrive on it. Peak performance stress provides us with vital information about ourselves, and stimulates activity, enhances creativity, and motivates us to live happy and fulfilling lives. Drawing on her experience as a counsellor, stress management and assertiveness trainer, Jan Sutton not only equips you with easily mastered strategies for conquering negative stress, she also offers you a personal development programme for building self-esteem and self-confidence. Supported by comprehensive case studies, illustrations, and practical activities, this book supplies you with a range of techniques that can positively transform your life. Jan Sutton (Dip CPC) is co-author (with William Stewart) of *Learning to Counsel* in this series.

192pp. illus. 1 85703 238 1.

BUILDING SELF-ESTEEM
How to replace self-doubt with confidence and well-being

William Stewart

Low self-esteem results from our attaching negative values to ourselves. Its effects are critical and influence almost every aspect of our lives. High self-esteem is positive. It is linked to optimism and the ability to exert some control over events. People who improve their self-esteem find that their lives take on new meaning as confidence grows and well-being is enhanced. This practical, self-help book reveals how the ravages of faulty beliefs about self can be reversed, enabling the reader to develop a firm belief in his or her attributes, accomplishments and abilities. Through a series of exercises and case studies it provides strategies for building self-esteem; it will help readers set clear goals and work steadily towards them. *Building Self-Esteem* is also a valuable handbook for those who work in healthcare and counselling. William Stewart is a freelance counsellor, supervisor and author. His background is in nursing, psychiatric social work and four years as a student counsellor and lecturer at a London college of nursing.

160pp. illus. 1 85703 251 9.

MANAGING YOUR PERSONAL FINANCES
How to achieve financial security and survive the shrinking welfare state

John Claxton

Life for most people has become increasingly beset by financial worries, and meanwhile the once-dependable prop of state help is shrinking. Today's financial world is a veritable jungle full of predators after your money. This book will help you to check your financial health and prepare a strategy towards creating your own welfare state and financial independence. Find out in simple language with many examples and case studies how to avoid debt, how to finance your home, how to prepare for possible incapacity or redundancy and how to finance your retirement, including care in old age. Discover how to acquire new financial skills, increase your income, reduce outgoings, and prepare to survive in a more self-reliant world. John Claxton is a chartered management accountant and chartered secretary; he teaches personal money management in adult education.

160pp. illus. 1 85703 328 0.

LEARNING TO COUNSEL
How to develop the skills to work effectively with others

Jan Sutton and William Stewart

Counselling skills are not only used by professional counsellors – they are relevant to a wide range of people as part of their work. They can also enhance all relationships. This practical book presents the principles of counselling and the fundamental skills involved. It is arranged in a logical sequence with exercises to work through and case studies to follow throughout the book. It is a must if you want to learn how to improve the quality of your relationships and gain insight into both the counselling process and yourself. Jan Sutton is an independent counsellor, trainer, author and personal development consultant. She facilitates counselling and related topics for the University of Southampton and various adult education departments. William Stewart is a freelance counsellor, counsellor supervisor, and author whose background is nursing, psychiatric social work and four years as a student counsellor/lecturer.

160pp. illus. 1 85703 229 2.

BUYING A PERSONAL COMPUTER
How to choose the right equipment to meet your needs

Allen Brown

Many thousands of personal computers (PCs) are sold annually and they are becoming general purpose everyday tools. However PC technology has been advancing year by year and there is a problem relating to the widening knowledge gap between user/buyer and the PC. Buying a PC for the first time will represent, to many people, a significant financial outlay. This book will help potential buyers in their choice of PC, their selection of peripherals, choosing appropriate software, bridging the knowledge gap between the PC and its buyer/owner/user, and discovering what the full potential of the PC is. It aims to be precise yet with sufficient information to enable a new user to understand a PC specification and to ensure that it will be adequate for their needs. It will also provide information on applications that the buyer may be thinking of for the future. Dr Allen Brown lectures in electronics at Anglia Polytechnic University.

160pp. illus. 1 85703 233 0. 2nd edition.

MAKING A COMPLAINT
How to put your case successfully and win redress

Helen Shay

Whether you've bought faulty shoes or been sold an unsuitable investment; been over-charged by a bank or suffered the holiday from hell; this book guides you through the maze of complaints procedures, courts, ombudsmen and other forms of consumer redress. It makes the law user-friendly and shows you how to obtain compensation – fast. It shows the way to cut through the aggravation and achieve the best solution for you. Helen Shay is a solicitor of twelve years' standing. She has worked both in private practice and as an in-house lawyer for a major high street retailer – so has experience of consumer disputes from both sides. Currently with an ombudsman's office, she is well-versed in current consumer issues and the problems which can confront the individual versus large organisations. She also tutors and lectures part-time in commercial law, and is knowledgeable in contract, consumer credit, banking law, conveyancing and other legal areas affecting everyday life.

160pp. illus. 1 85703 102 4.

CHOOSING A PACKAGE HOLIDAY
How to plan and prepare for a disaster-free experience

Christine Miller

Whether you are going abroad for the first time or are an experienced traveller, this book provides valuable and unbiased information on all aspects of package holidays. By being well briefed before entering the travel agency, you will get the most out of your travel agent and ultimately your holiday. This book shows you how to prepare, step-by-step. It guides you through the minefield of choosing and booking a holiday, taking out appropriate insurance cover, sorting out car hire, obtaining passports and foreign currency, dealing effectively with problems and complaints, and making insurance claims if things go wrong. Do you actually stand to gain anything from special offers and agent's discounts? These and many other subjects are covered to help you make the right holiday choices. Christine Miller has 11 years' experience of working in travel agencies and dealing with all aspects of package holidays. She has travelled extensively both in Europe and worldwide.

144pp. illus. 1 85703 332 9.

TEACHING SOMEONE TO DRIVE
How to prepare a learner driver safely and successfully for the driving test

Angela Oatridge

Accompanying a learner driver safely is often a frightening experience for both pupil and instructor. Like learning to read, driving is one of those skills which we do automatically, so it is not always easy to explain exactly what to do, and why. This book is aimed at anyone who is going to sit beside a learner driver. It answers such questions as how to explain a sequence of actions, why we do certain actions, what to do if our learner panics, why a learner may not understand, and how to remain calm in all circumstances. A graduate of The Open University, Angela Oatridge has been a qualified Driving Instructor for twenty-five years. Besides running a successful driving school in England, Scotland and on the Continent, she has taught many people to become Driving Instructors and has lectured for many years on the subject of teaching driving. She has also written various articles and spoken on radio and television on driving tuition.

144pp. illus. 1 85703 343 4.

How To Books

How To Books provide practical help on a large range of topics. They are available through all good bookshops or can be ordered direct from the distributors. Just tick the titles you want and complete the form on the following page.

___ Apply to an Industrial Tribunal (£7.99)
___ Applying for a Job (£8.99)
___ Applying for a United States Visa (£15.99)
___ Backpacking Round Europe (£8.99)
___ Be a Freelance Journalist (£8.99)
___ Be a Freelance Secretary (£8.99)
___ Become a Freelance Sales Agent (£9.99)
___ Becoming a Father (£8.99)
___ Buy & Run a Shop (£8.99)
___ Buy & Run a Small Hotel (£8.99)
___ Buying a Personal Computer (£9.99)
___ Career Networking (£8.99)
___ Career Planning for Women (£8.99)
___ Cash from your Computer (£9.99)
___ Choosing a Nursing Home (£9.99)
___ Choosing a Package Holiday (£8.99)
___ Claim State Benefits (£9.99)
___ Collecting a Debt (£9.99)
___ Communicate at Work (£7.99)
___ Conduct Staff Appraisals (£7.99)
___ Conducting Effective Interviews (£8.99)
___ Coping with Self Assessment (£9.99)
___ Copyright & Law for Writers (£8.99)
___ Counsel People at Work (£7.99)
___ Creating a Twist in the Tale (£8.99)
___ Creative Writing (£9.99)
___ Critical Thinking for Students (£8.99)
___ Dealing with a Death in the Family (£9.99)
___ Do Your Own Advertising (£8.99)
___ Do Your Own PR (£8.99)
___ Doing Business Abroad (£10.99)
___ Doing Business on the Internet (£12.99)
___ Doing Voluntary Work Abroad (£9.99)
___ Emigrate (£9.99)
___ Employ & Manage Staff (£8.99)
___ Find Temporary Work Abroad (£8.99)
___ Finding a Job in Canada (£9.99)
___ Finding a Job in Computers (£8.99)
___ Finding a Job in New Zealand (£9.99)
___ Finding a Job with a Future (£8.99)
___ Finding Work Overseas (£9.99)
___ Freelance DJ-ing (£8.99)
___ Freelance Teaching & Tutoring (£9.99)
___ Get a Job Abroad (£10.99)
___ Get a Job in Europe (£9.99)
___ Get a Job in France (£9.99)
___ Get a Job in Travel & Tourism (£8.99)
___ Get into Radio (£8.99)
___ Getting a Job in America (£10.99)
___ Getting a Job in Australia (£9.99)
___ Getting into Films & Television (£10.99)
___ Getting That Job (£8.99)
___ Getting your First Job (£8.99)
___ Going to University (£8.99)
___ Having a Baby (£8.99)

___ Helping your Child to Read (£8.99)
___ How to Study & Learn (£8.99)
___ Investing in People (£9.99)
___ Investing in Stocks & Shares (£9.99)
___ Keep Business Accounts (£7.99)
___ Know Your Rights at Work (£8.99)
___ Learning to Counsel (£9.99)
___ Live & Work in Germany (£9.99)
___ Live & Work in Greece (£9.99)
___ Live & Work in Italy (£8.99)
___ Live & Work in Portugal (£9.99)
___ Live & Work in the Gulf (£9.99)
___ Living & Working in America (£12.99)
___ Living & Working in Australia (£12.99)
___ Living & Working in Britain (£8.99)
___ Living & Working in China (£9.99)
___ Living & Working in Hong Kong (£10.99)
___ Living & Working in Israel (£10.99)
___ Living & Work in New Zealand (£9.99)
___ Living & Working in Saudi Arabia (£12.99)
___ Living & Working in the Netherlands (£9.99)
___ Living Away From Home (£8.99)
___ Making a Complaint (£8.99)
___ Making a Video (£9.99)
___ Making a Wedding Speech (£8.99)
___ Manage a Sales Team (£8.99)
___ Manage an Office (£8.99)
___ Manage Computers at Work (£8.99)
___ Manage People at Work (£8.99)
___ Manage Your Career (£8.99)
___ Managing Budgets & Cash Flows (£9.99)
___ Managing Credit (£8.99)
___ Managing Meetings (£8.99)
___ Managing Projects (£8.99)
___ Managing Your Personal Finances (£8.99)
___ Managing Yourself (£8.99)
___ Market Yourself (£8.99)
___ Mastering Book-Keeping (£8.99)
___ Mastering Business English (£8.99)
___ Master GCSE Accounts (£8.99)
___ Master Public Speaking (£8.99)
___ Migrating to Canada (£12.99)
___ Obtaining Visas & Work Permits (£9.99)
___ Organising Effective Training (£9.99)
___ Passing Exams Without Anxiety (£8.99)
___ Passing That Interview (£8.99)
___ Plan a Wedding (£8.99)
___ Planning Your Gap Year (£8.99)
___ Preparing a Business Plan (£8.99)
___ Publish a Book (£9.99)
___ Publish a Newsletter (£9.99)
___ Raise Funds & Sponsorship (£7.99)
___ Rent & Buy Property in France (£9.99)
___ Rent & Buy Property in Italy (£9.99)
___ Research Methods (£8.99)

___ Retire Abroad (£8.99)
___ Return to Work (£7.99)
___ Run a Voluntary Group (£8.99)
___ Setting up Home in Florida (£9.99)
___ Setting Up Your Own Limited Company (£9.99)
___ Spending a Year Abroad (£8.99)
___ Start a Business from Home (£7.99)
___ Start a New Career (£6.99)
___ Starting to Manage (£8.99)
___ Starting to Write (£8.99)
___ Start Word Processing (£8.99)
___ Start Your Own Business (£8.99)
___ Study Abroad (£8.99)
___ Study & Live in Britain (£7.99)
___ Studying at University (£8.99)
___ Studying for a Degree (£8.99)
___ Successful Grandparenting (£8.99)
___ Successful Mail Order Marketing (£9.99)
___ Successful Single Parenting (£8.99)
___ Survive Divorce (£8.99)
___ Surviving Redundancy (£8.99)
___ Taking in Students (£8.99)
___ Taking on Staff (£8.99)
___ Taking Your A-Levels (£8.99)
___ Teach Abroad (£8.99)
___ Teach Adults (£8.99)
___ Teaching Someone to Drive (£8.99)
___ Travel Round the World (£8.99)
___ Understand Finance at Work (£8.99)
___ Use a Library (£7.99)
___ Using the Internet (£9.99)

___ Winning Consumer Competitions (£8.99)
___ Winning Presentations (£8.99)
___ Work from Home (£8.99)
___ Work in an Office (£7.99)
___ Work in Retail (£8.99)
___ Work with Dogs (£8.99)
___ Working Abroad (£14.99)
___ Working as a Holiday Rep (£9.99)
___ Working as an Au Pair (£8.99)
___ Working in Japan (£10.99)
___ Working in Photography (£8.99)
___ Working in the Gulf (£10.99)
___ Working in Hotels & Catering (£9.99)
___ Working on Contract Worldwide (£9.99)
___ Working on Cruise Ships (£9.99)
___ Write a Press Release (£9.99)
___ Write & Sell Computer Software (£9.99)
___ Write for Television (£8.99)
___ Writing a CV that Works (£8.99)
___ Writing a Non Fiction Book (£9.99)
___ Writing a Report (£8.99)
___ Writing a Textbook (£12.99)
___ Writing an Assignment (£8.99)
___ Writing an Essay (£8.99)
___ Writing & Publishing Poetry (£9.99)
___ Writing & Selling a Novel (£8.99)
___ Writing Business Letters (£8.99)
___ Writing for Publication (£8.99)
___ Writing Reviews (£9.99)
___ Writing Romantic Fiction (£9.99)
___ Writing Science Fiction (£9.99)
___ Writing Your Dissertation (£8.99)

To: Plymbridge Distributors Ltd, Plymbridge House, Estover Road, Plymouth PL6 7PZ. Customer Services Tel: (01752) 202301. Fax: (01752) 202331.

Please send me copies of the titles I have indicated. Please add postage & packing (UK £1, Europe including Eire, £2, World £3 airmail).

☐ I enclose cheque/PO payable to Plymbridge Distributors Ltd for £

☐ Please charge to my ☐ MasterCard, ☐ Visa, ☐ AMEX card.

Account No.

Card Expiry Date ___ 19 ___ ☎ Credit Card orders may be faxed or phoned.

Customer Name (CAPITALS) ....

Address ....

.... Postcode ....

Telephone........................... Signature ....

Every effort will be made to despatch your copy as soon as possible but to avoid possible disappointment please allow up to 21 days for despatch time (42 days if overseas). Prices and availability are subject to change without notice.

Code BPA